Mandalas of the South West

An adult coloring book for relaxation and fun.

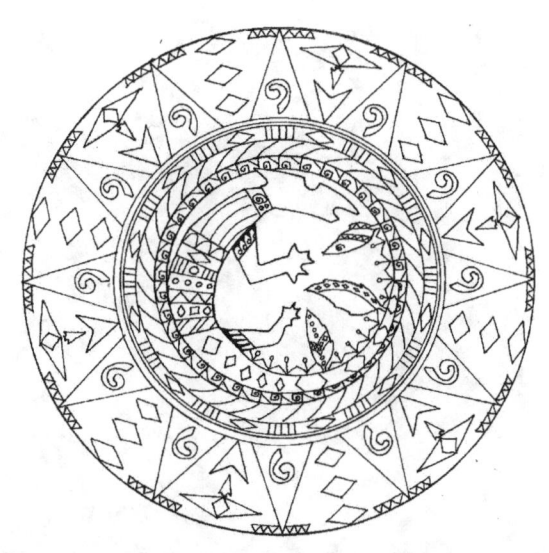

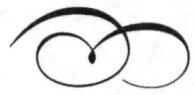

Illustrated by j. a. Christensen

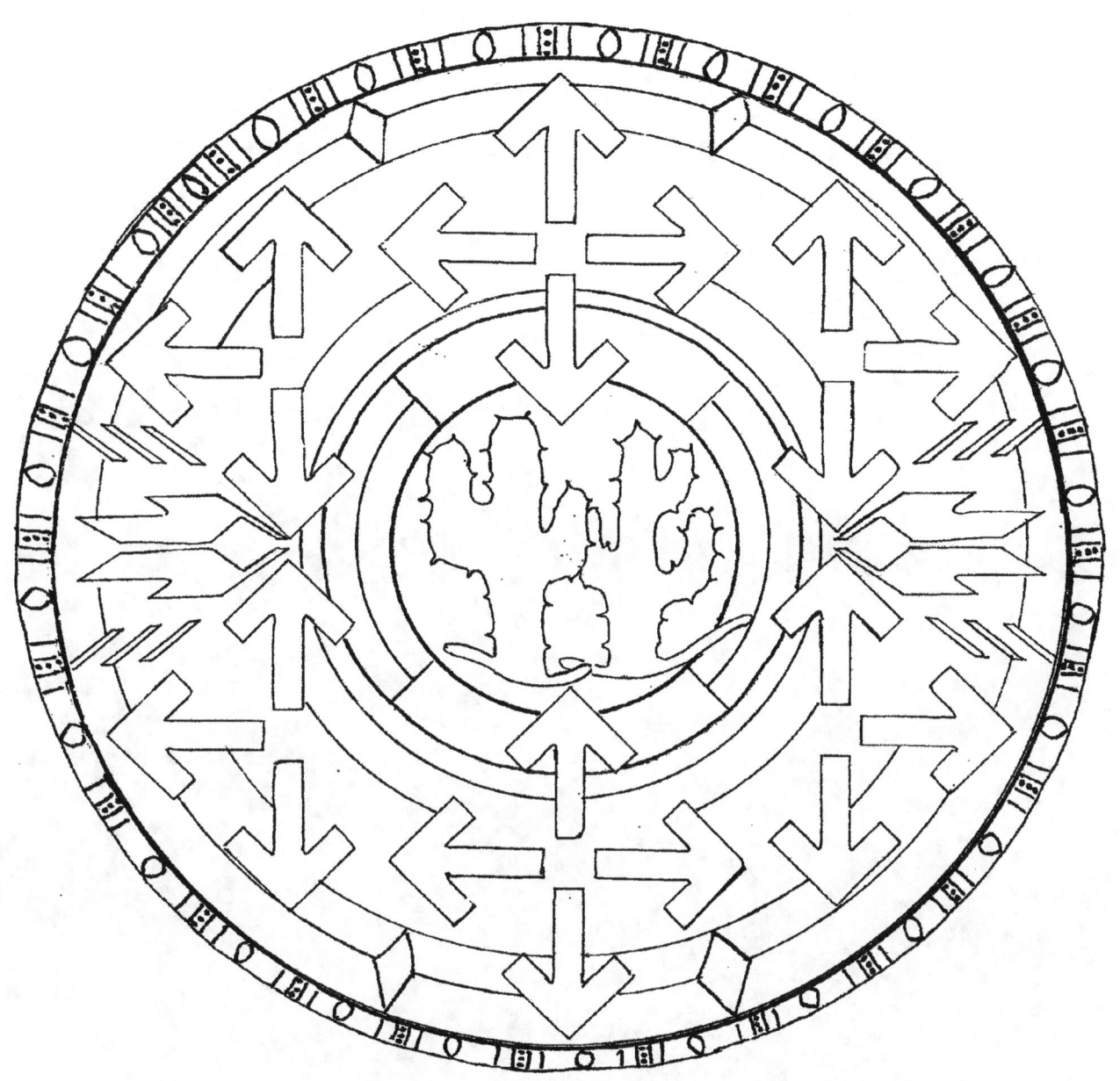

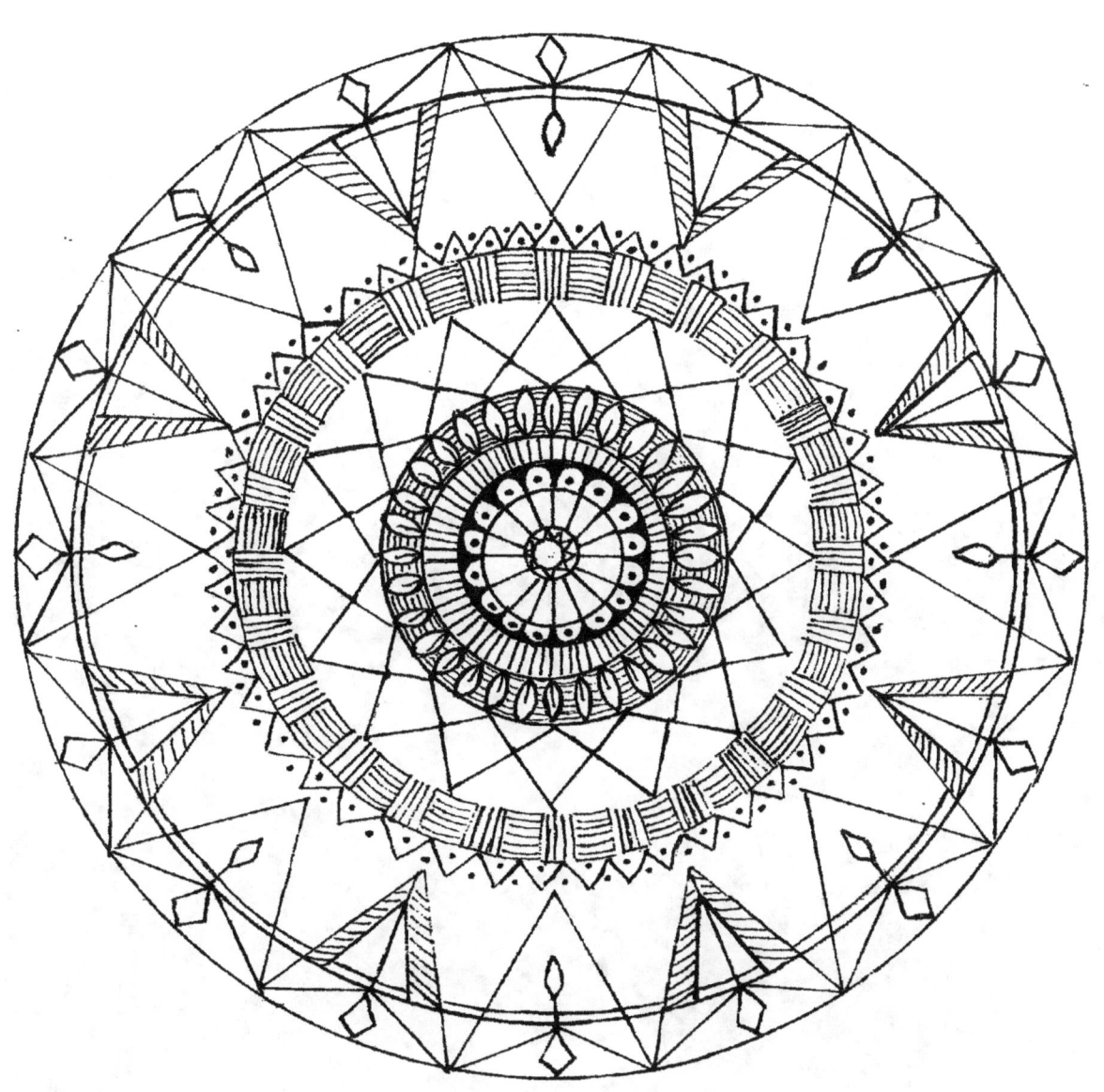

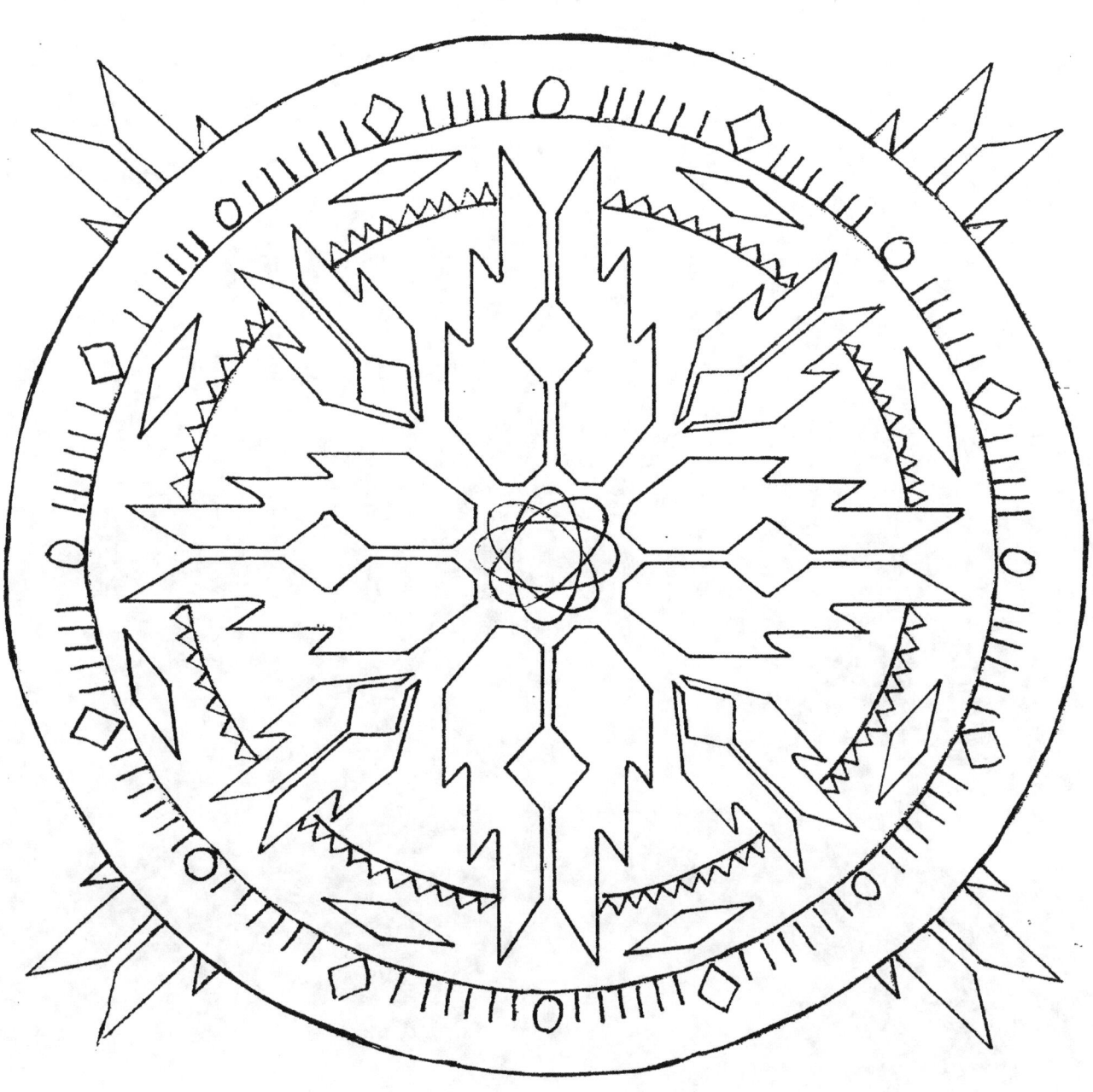

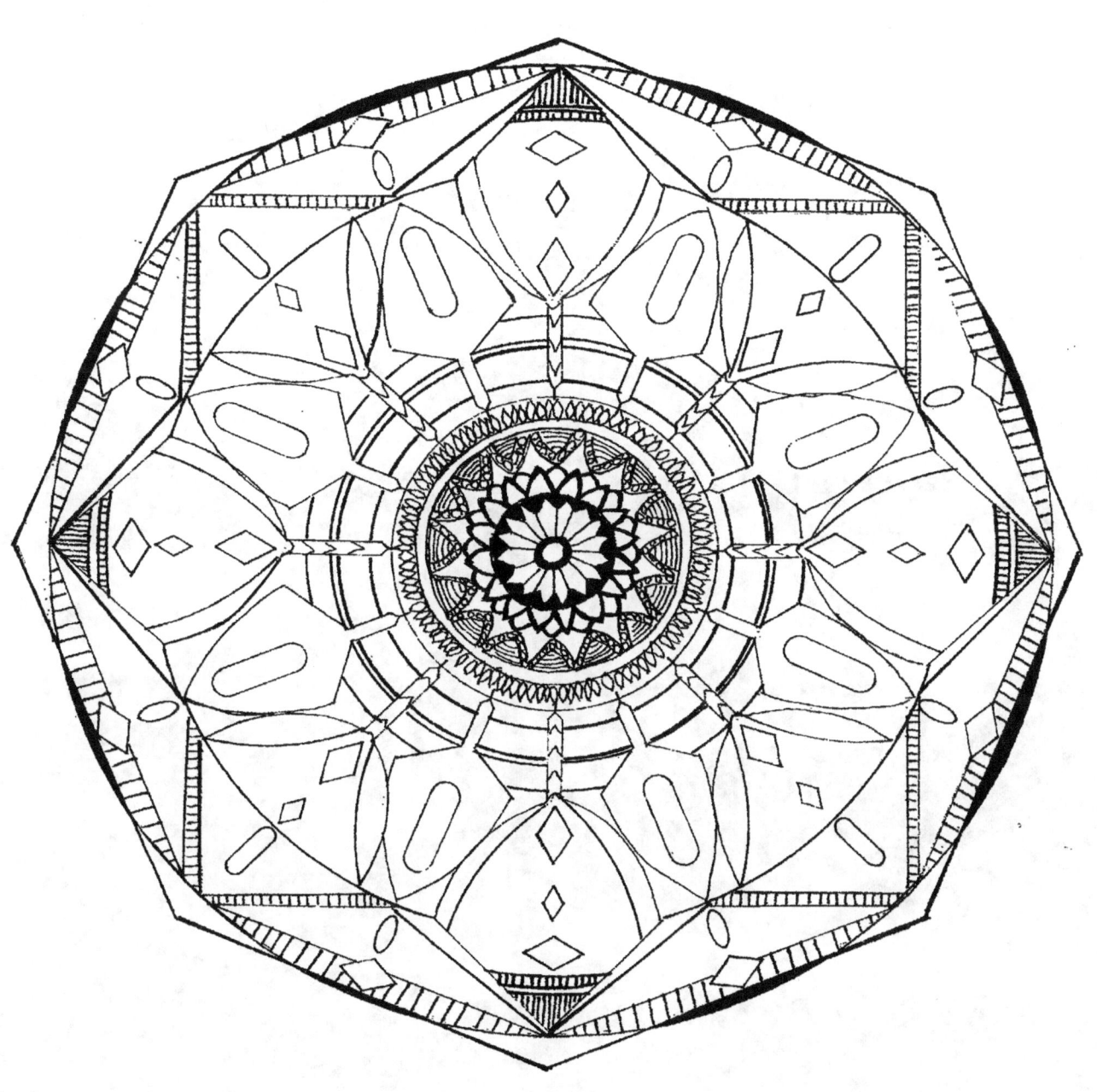

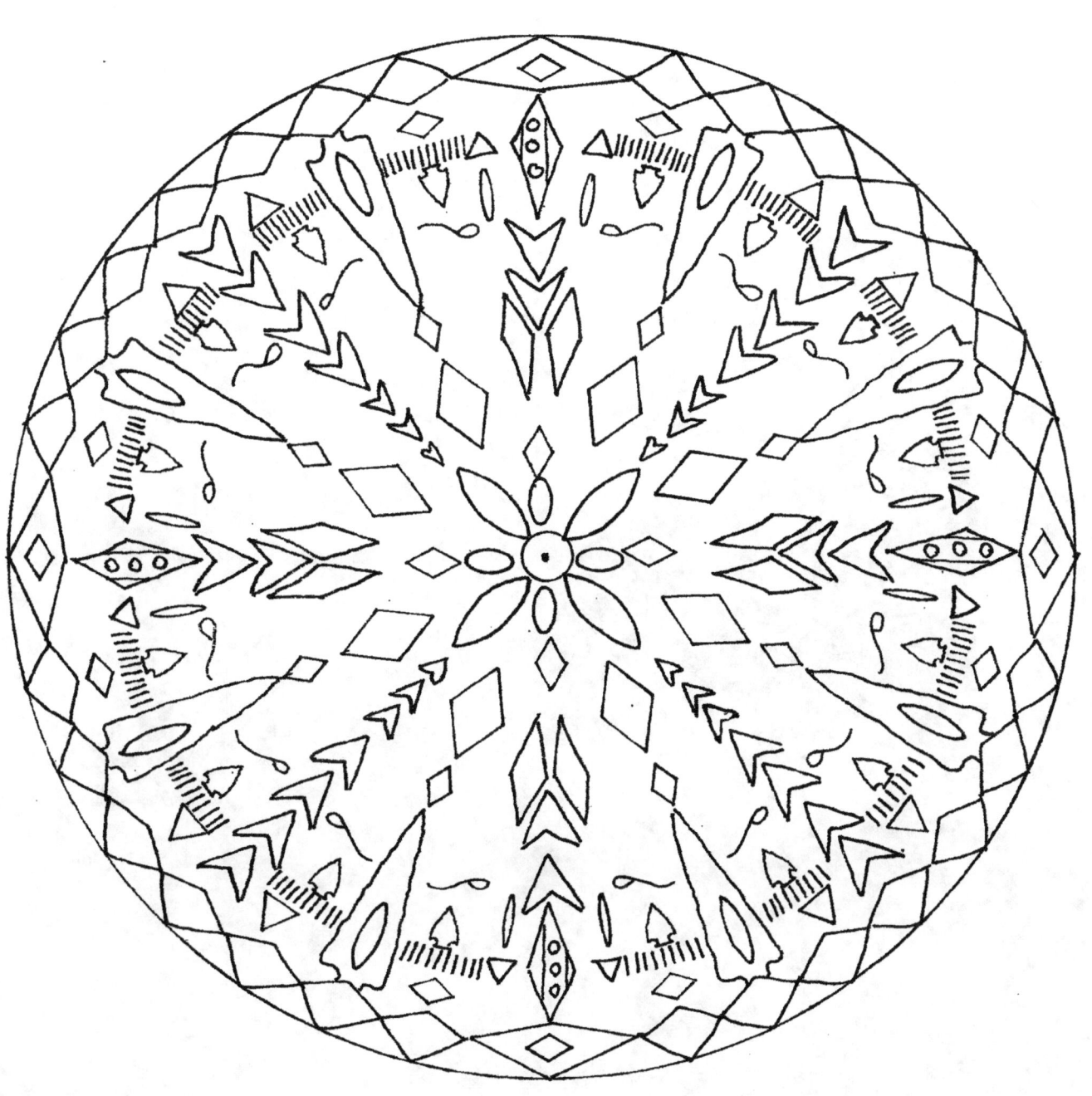

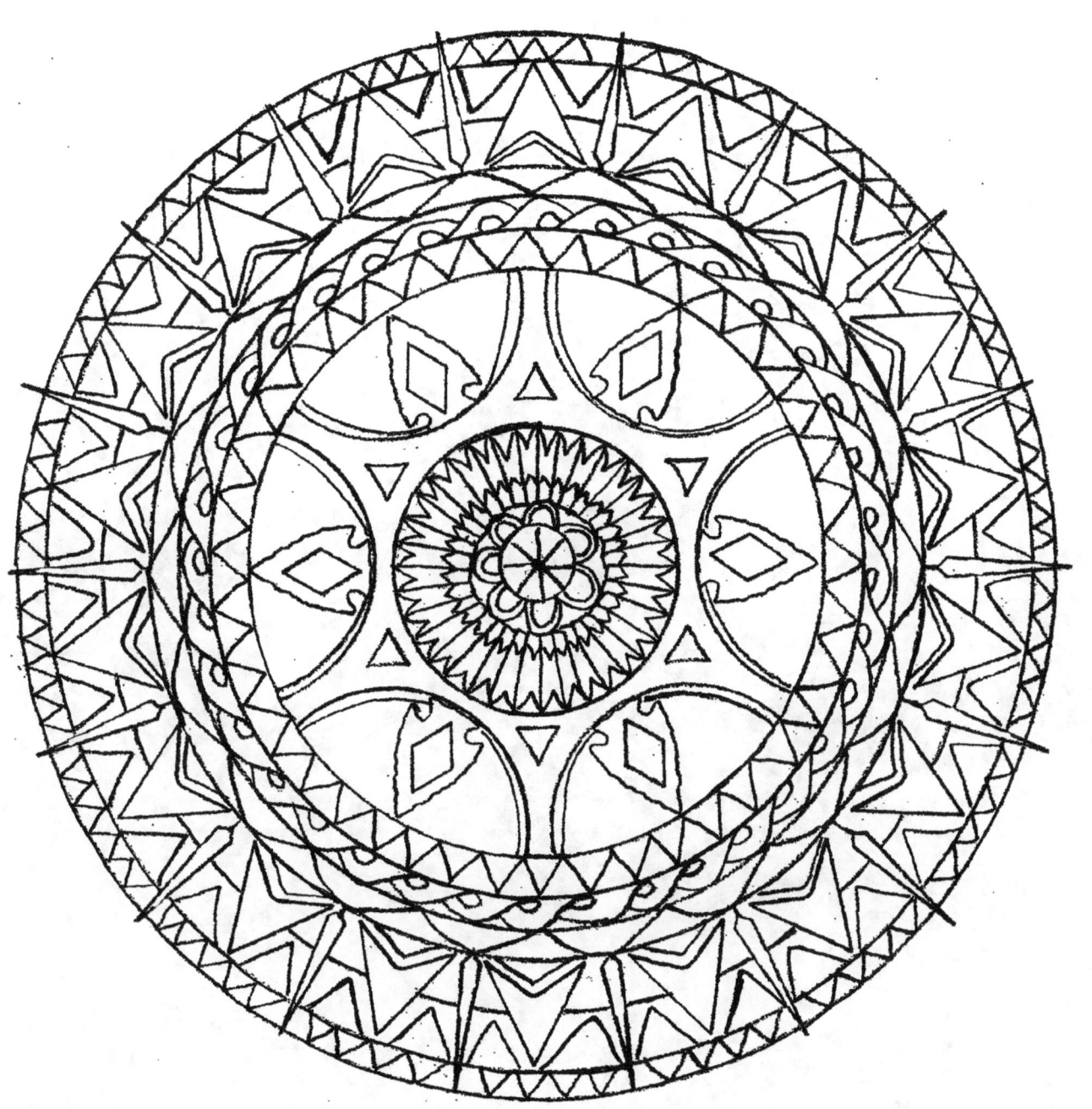

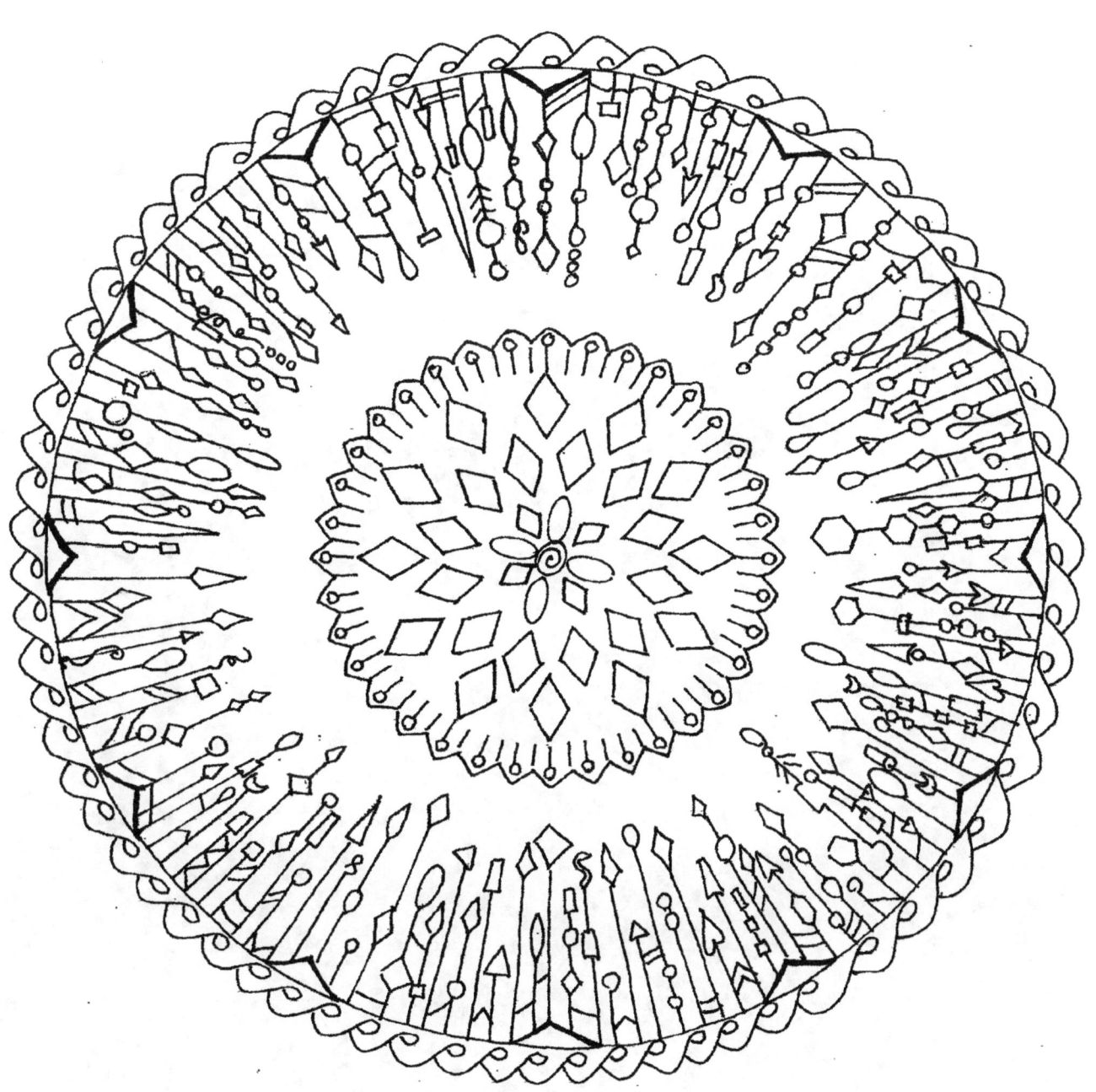

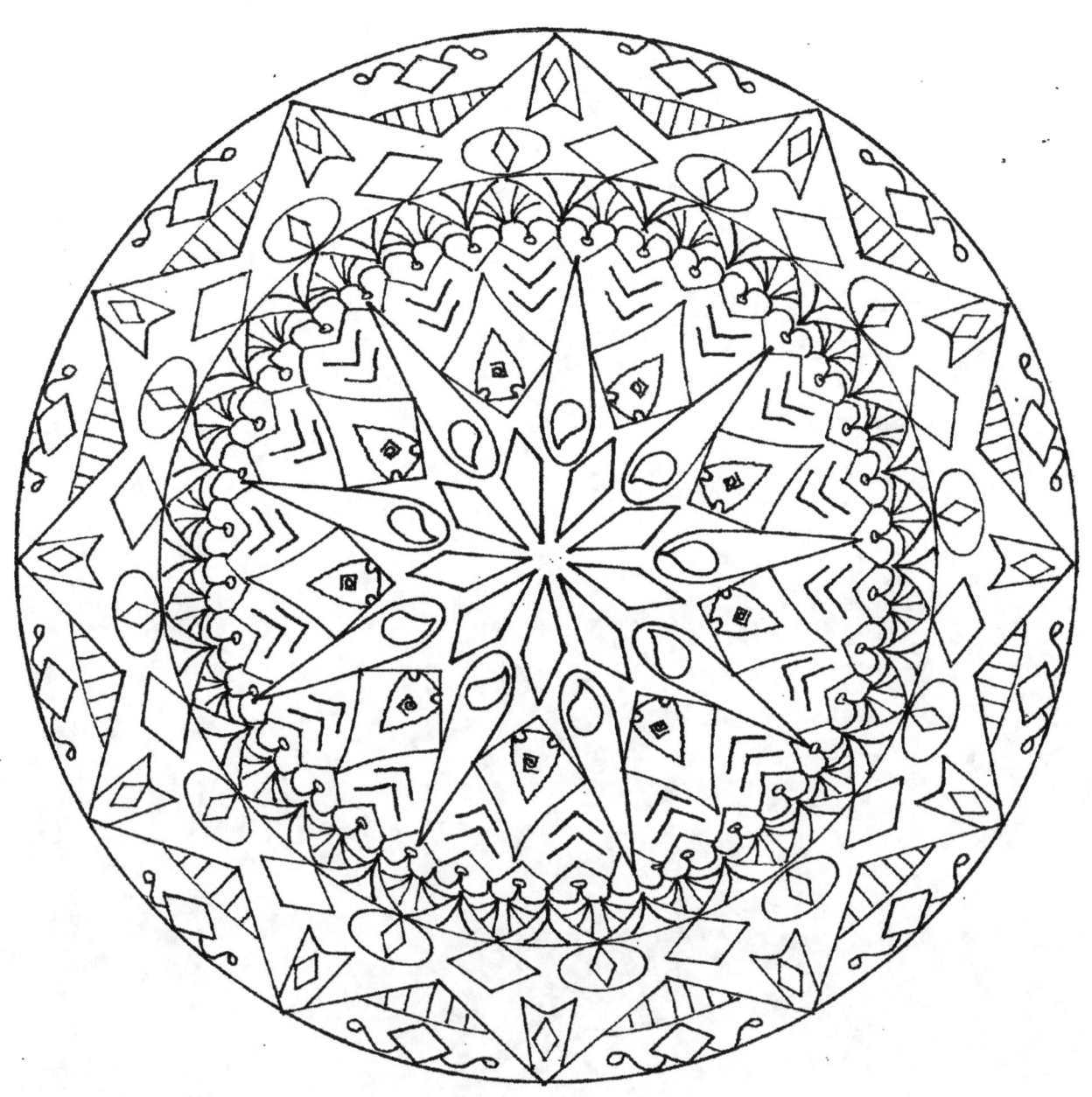

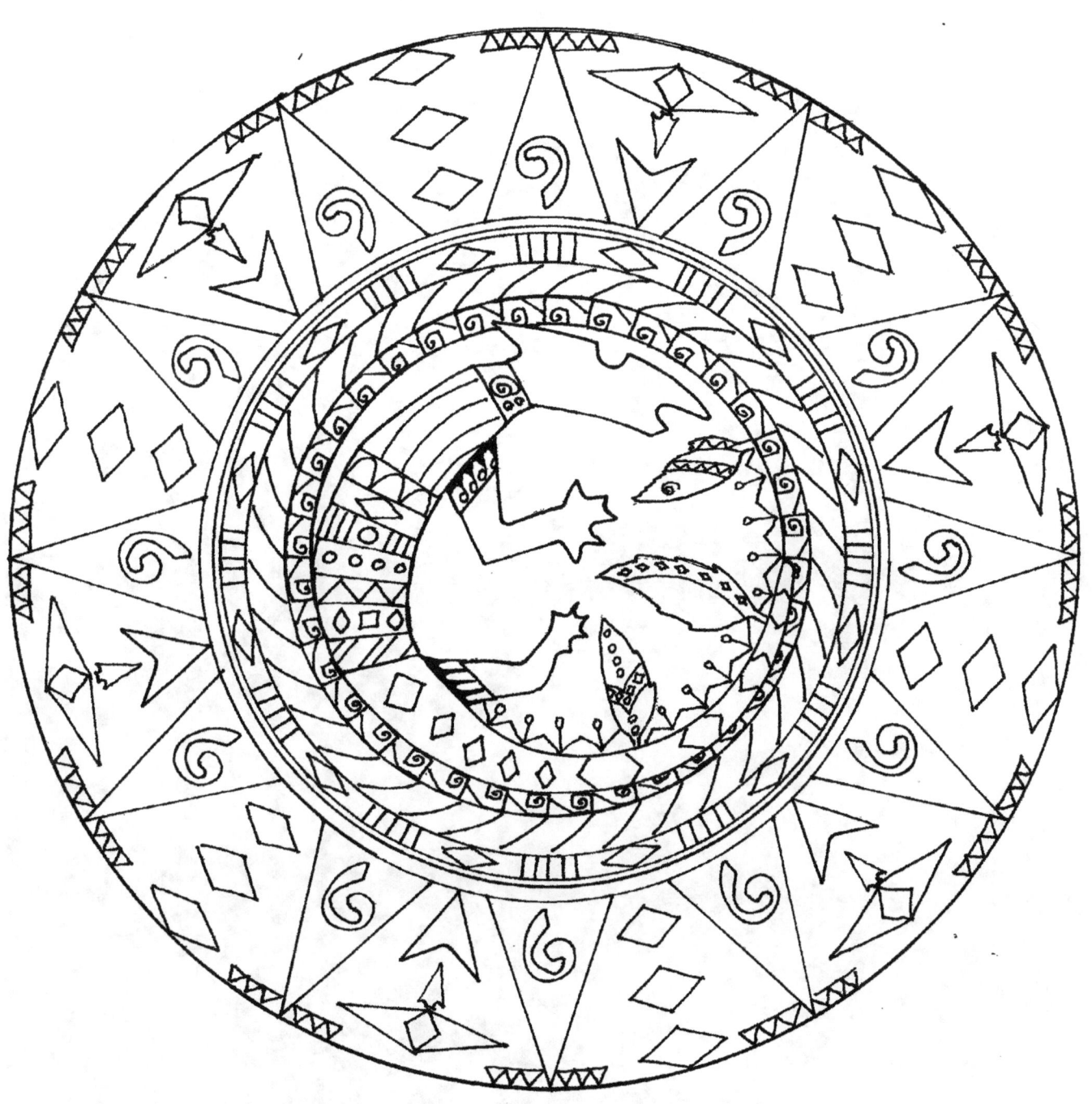

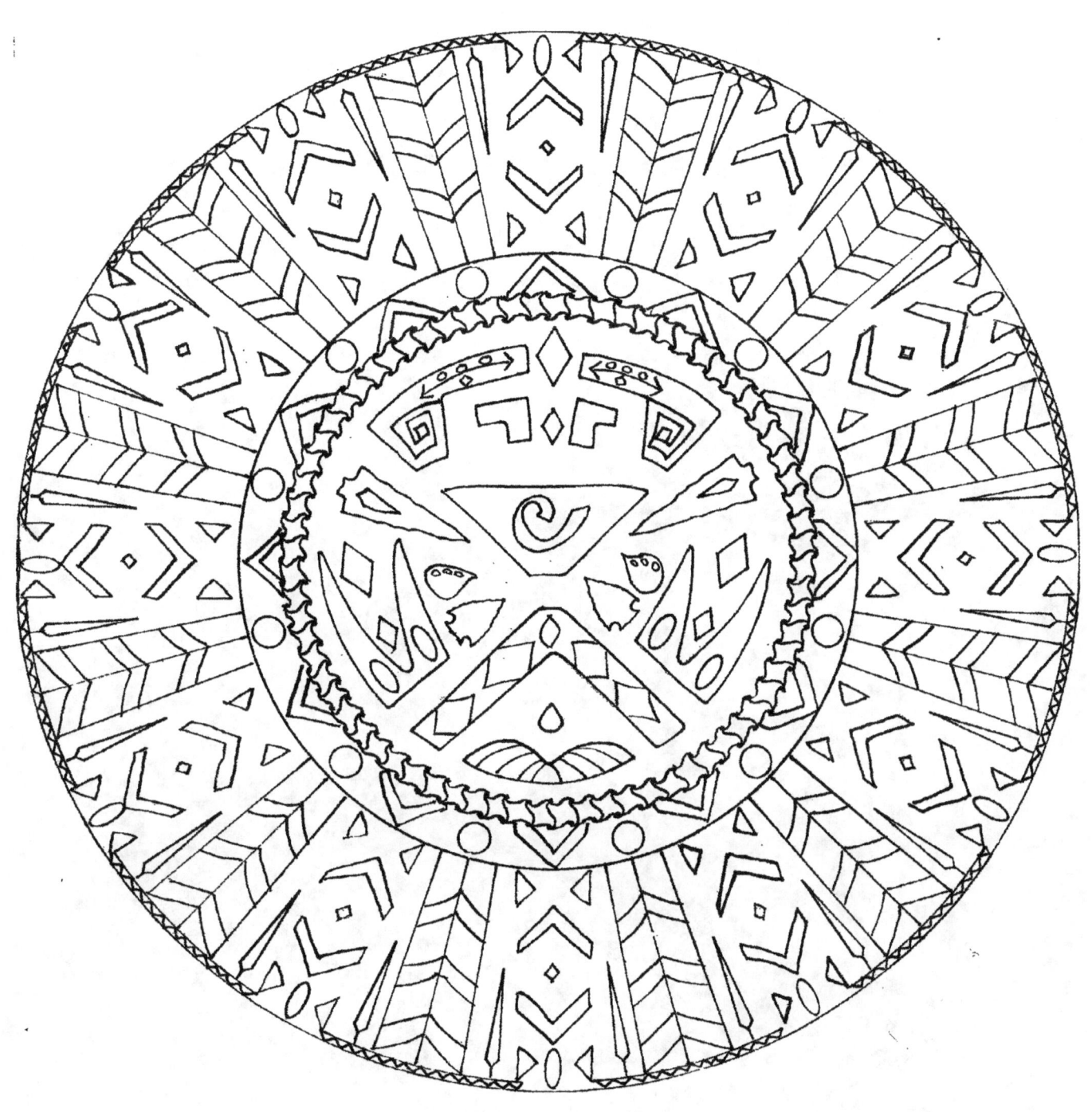

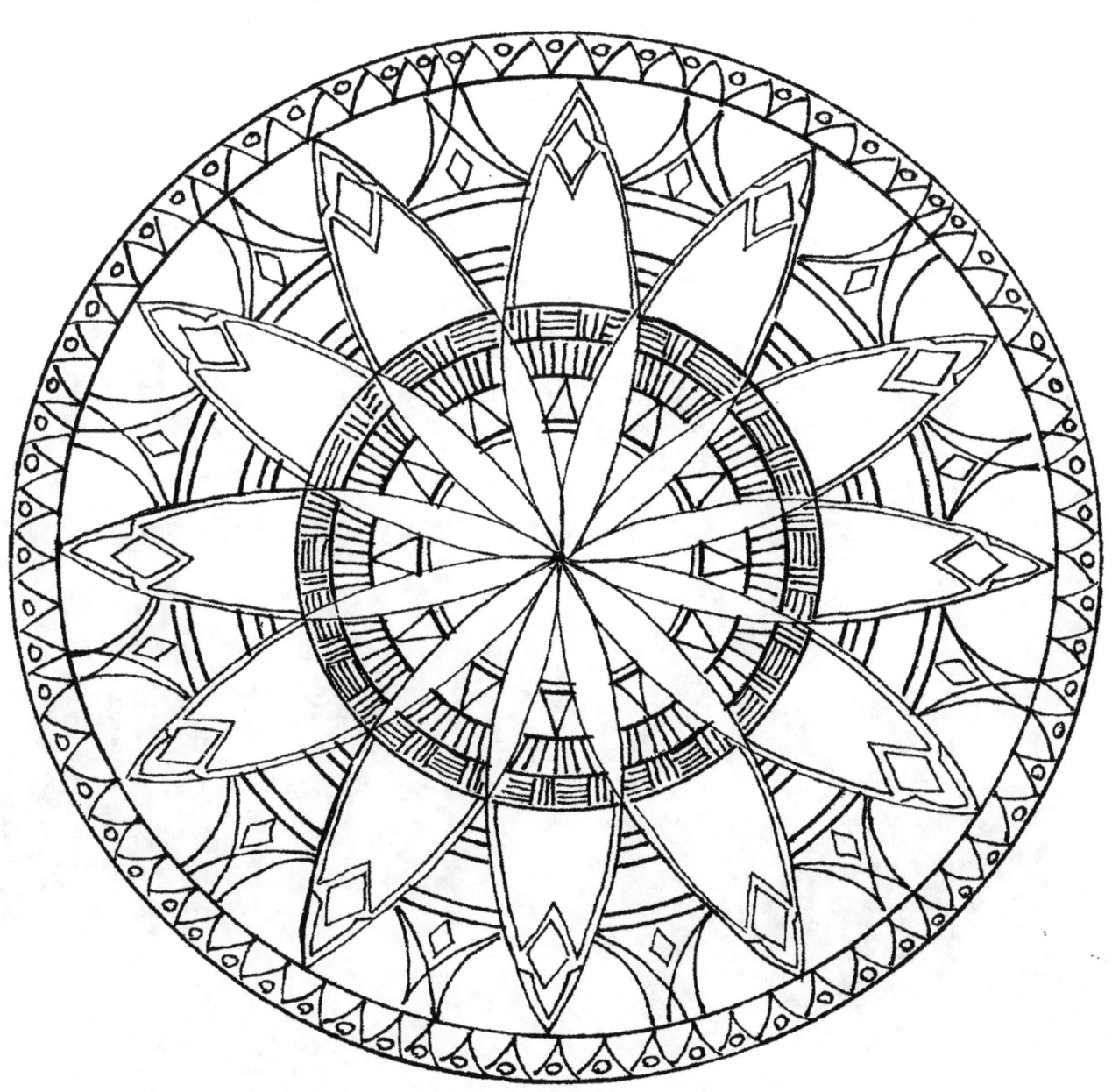

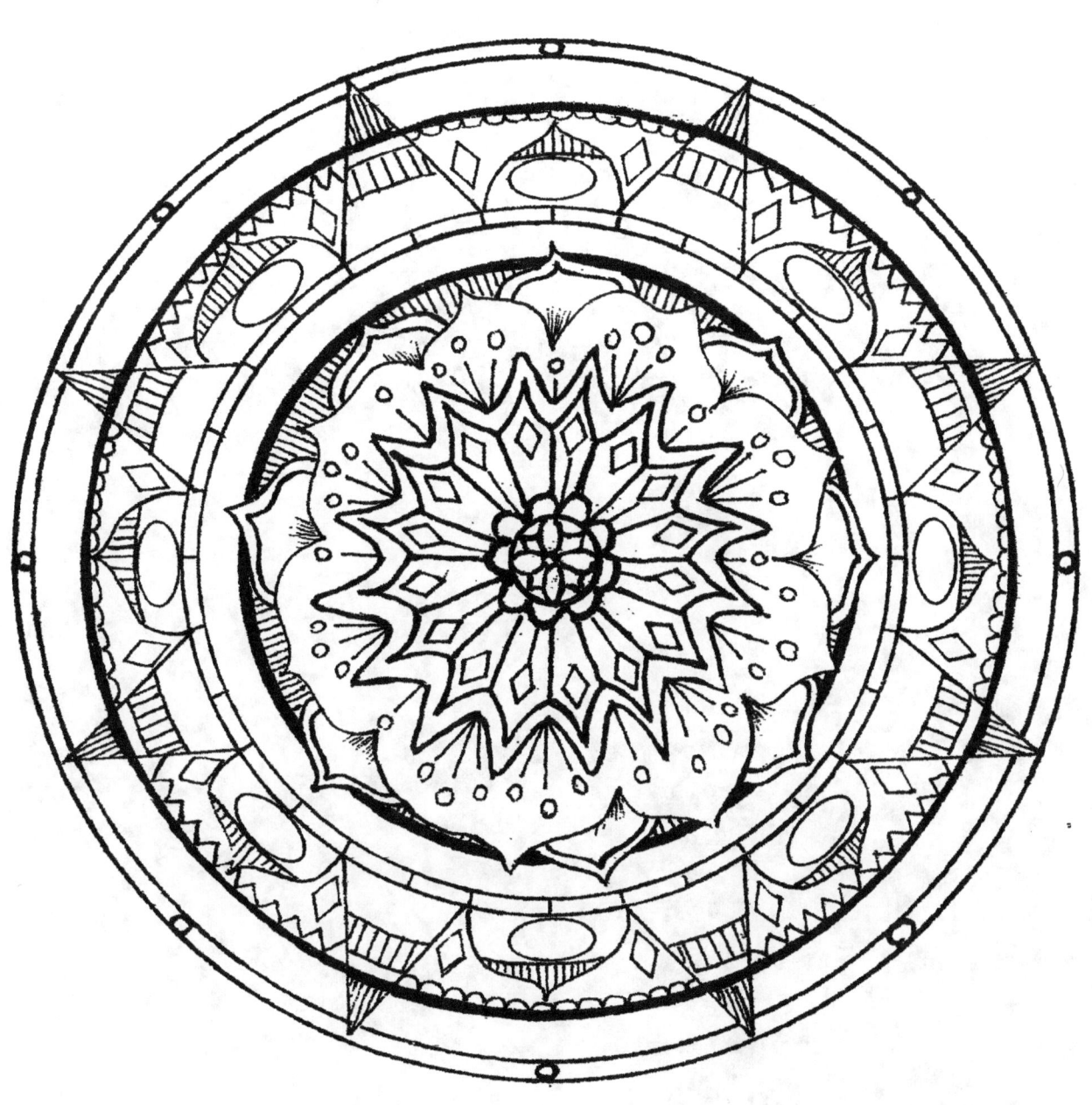

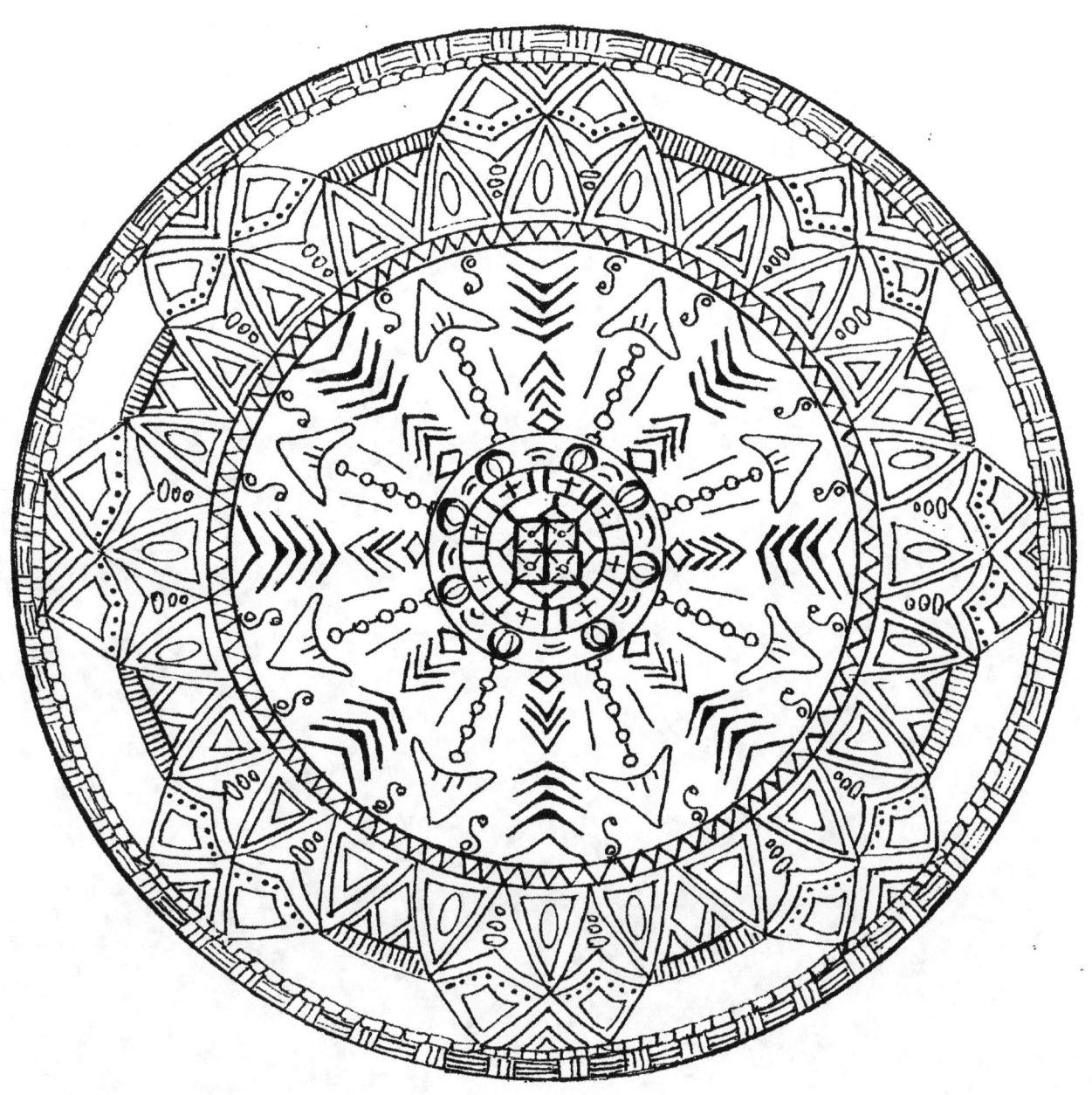

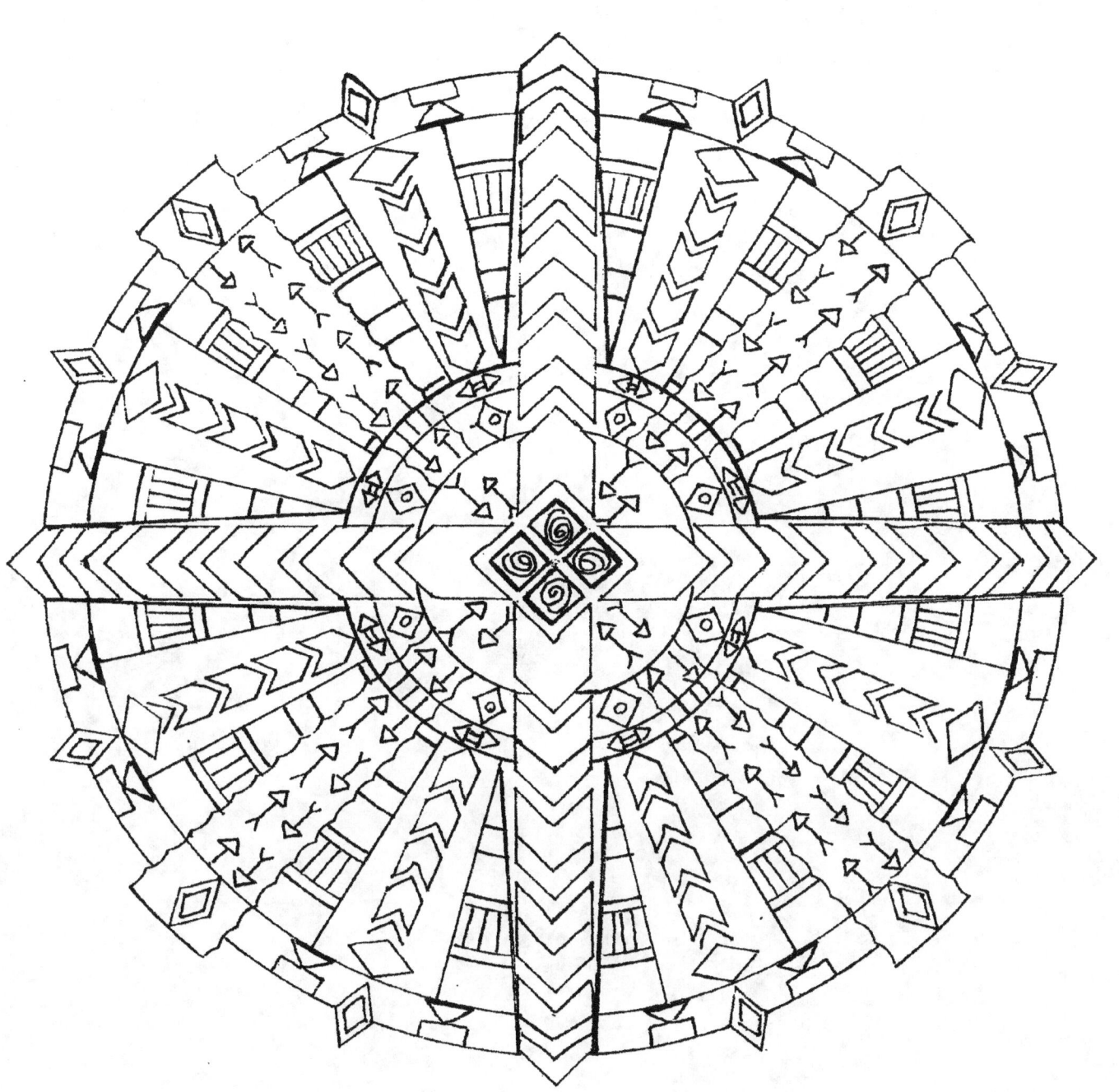

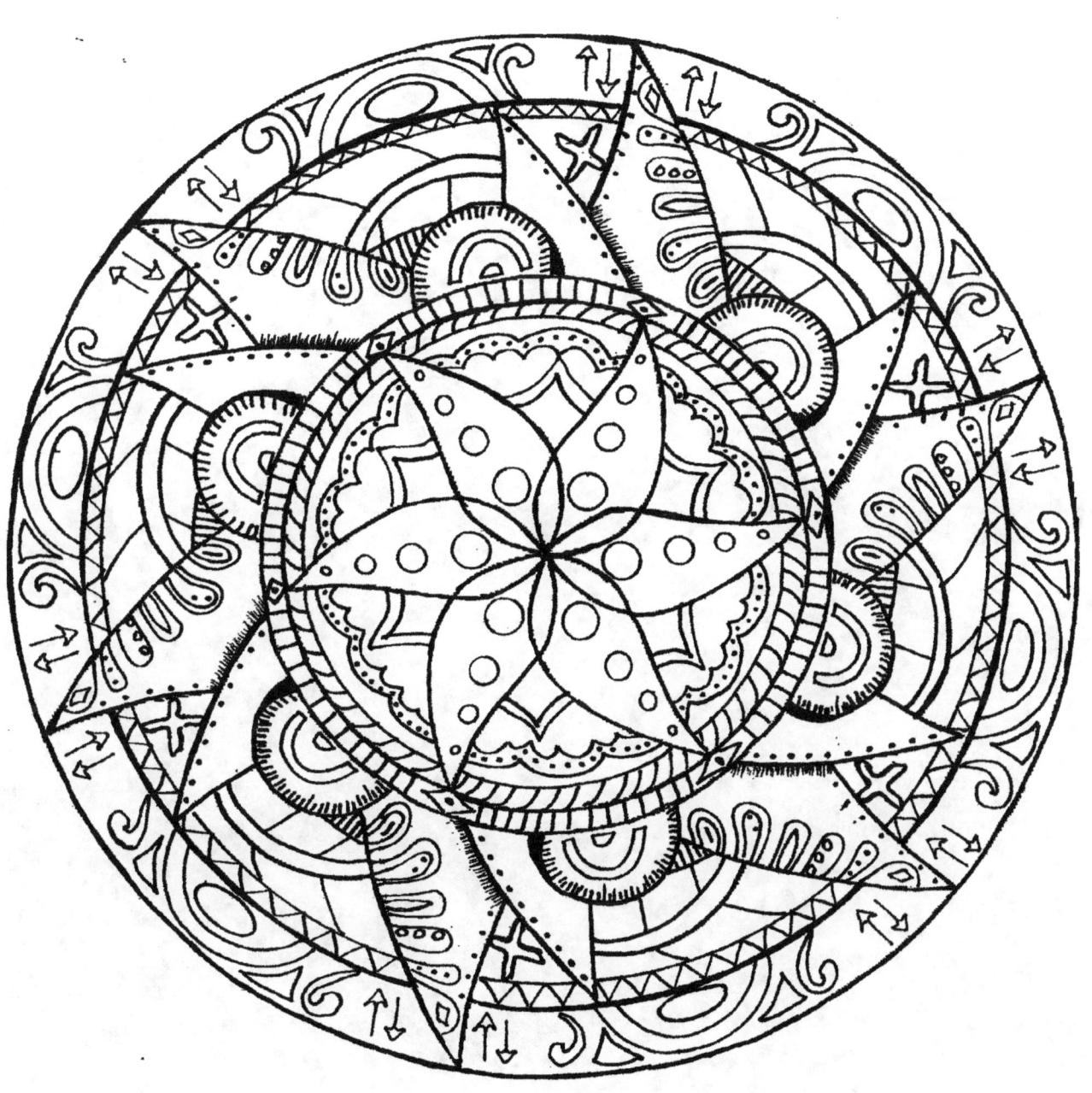

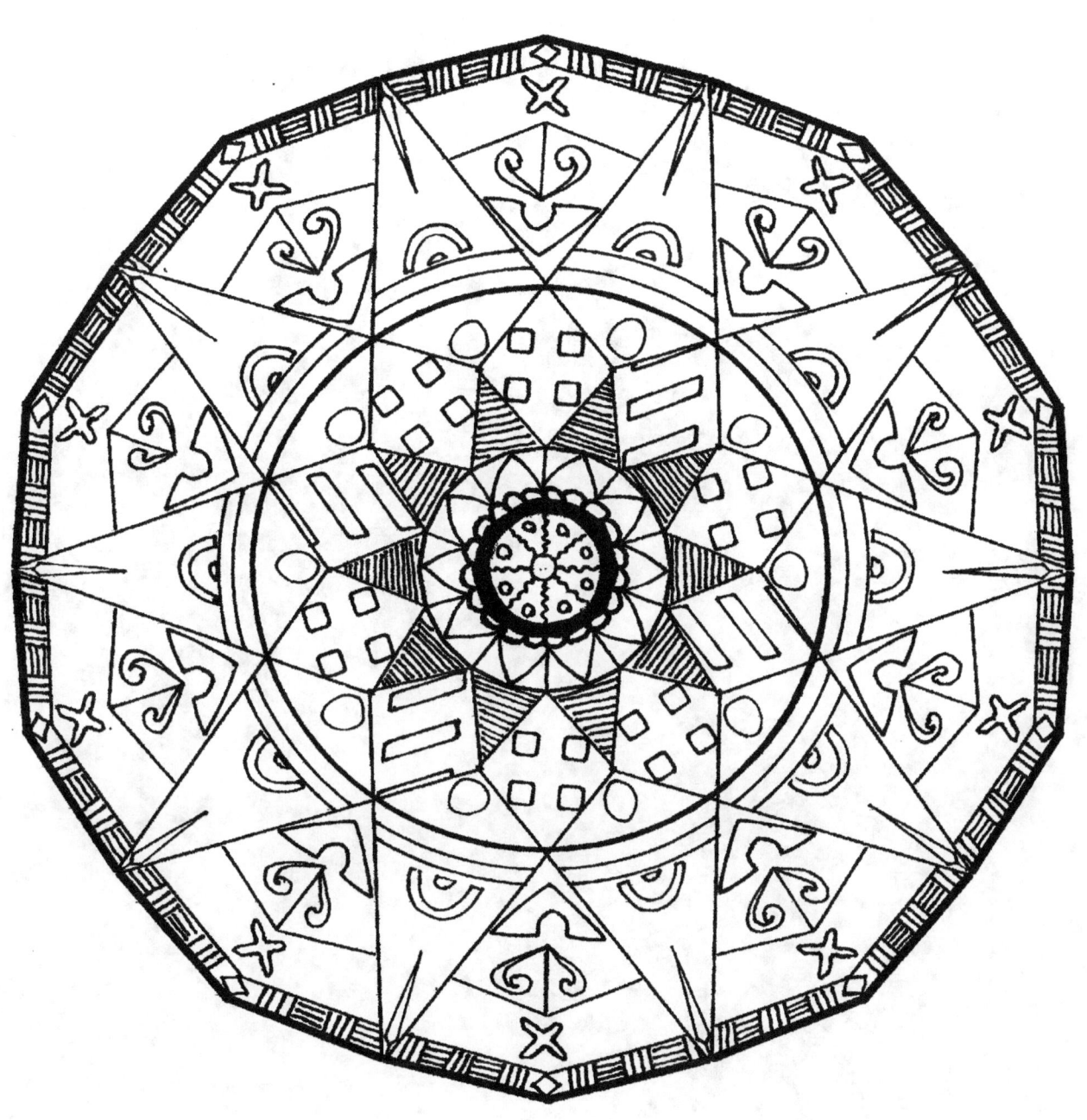

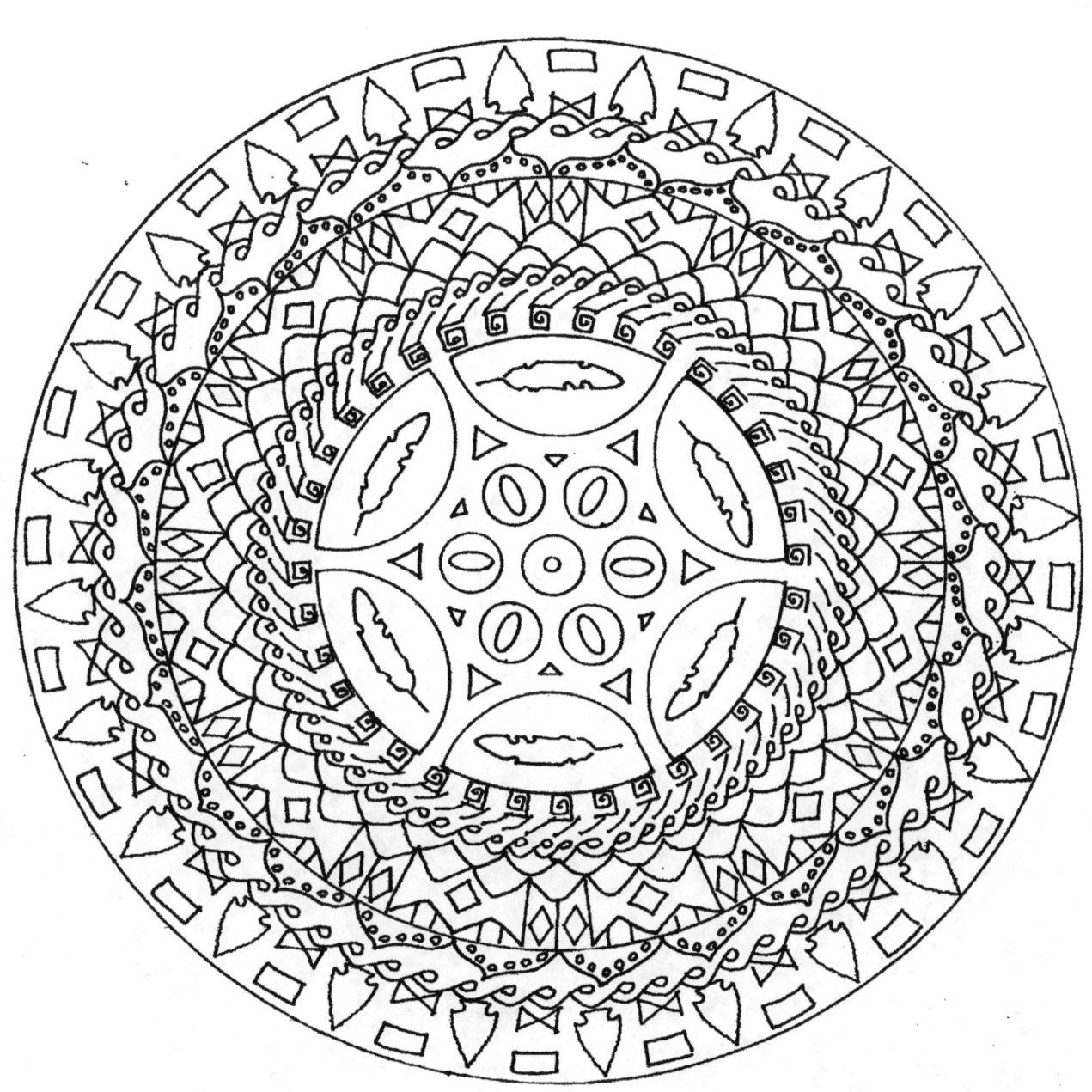

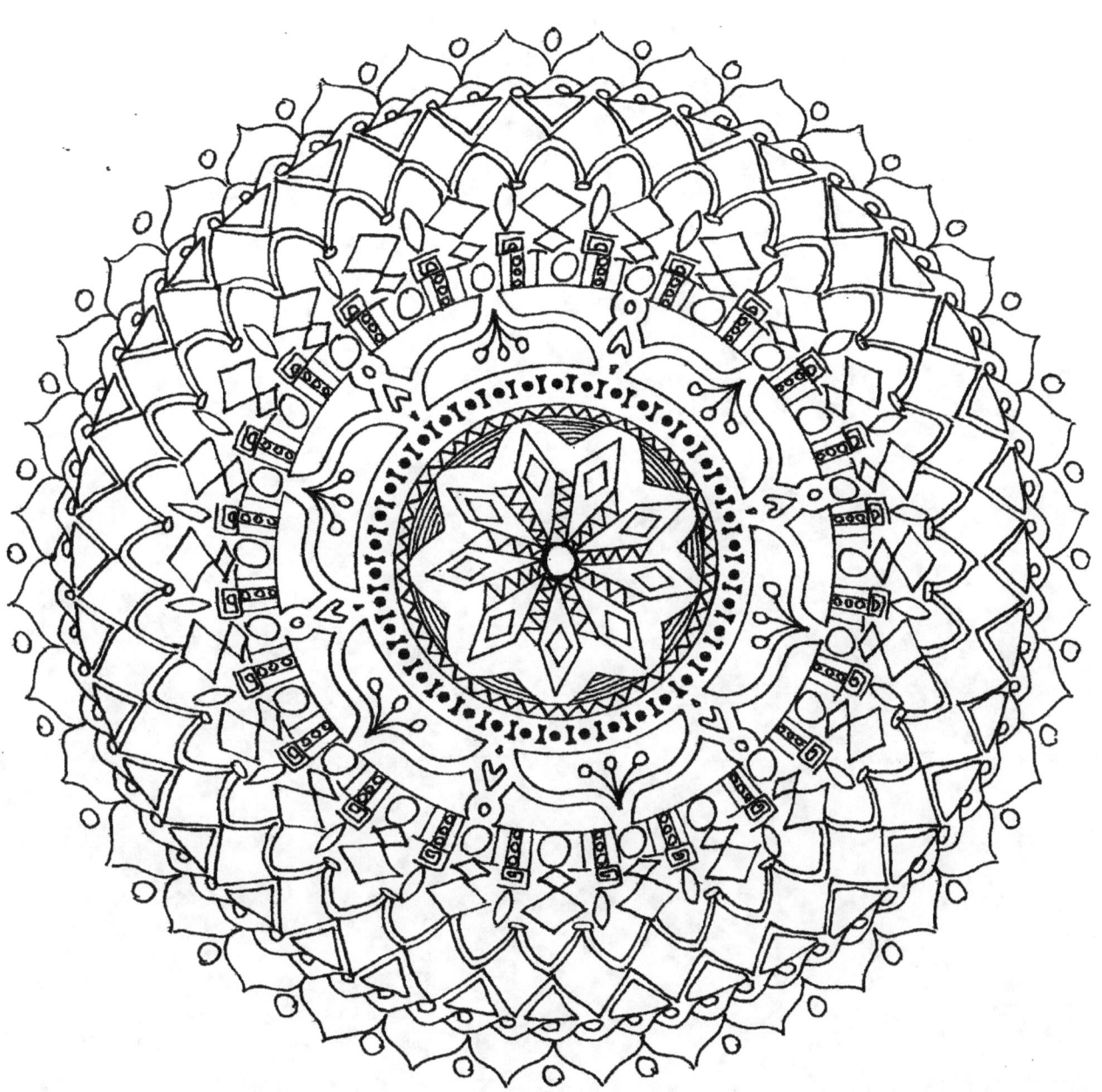

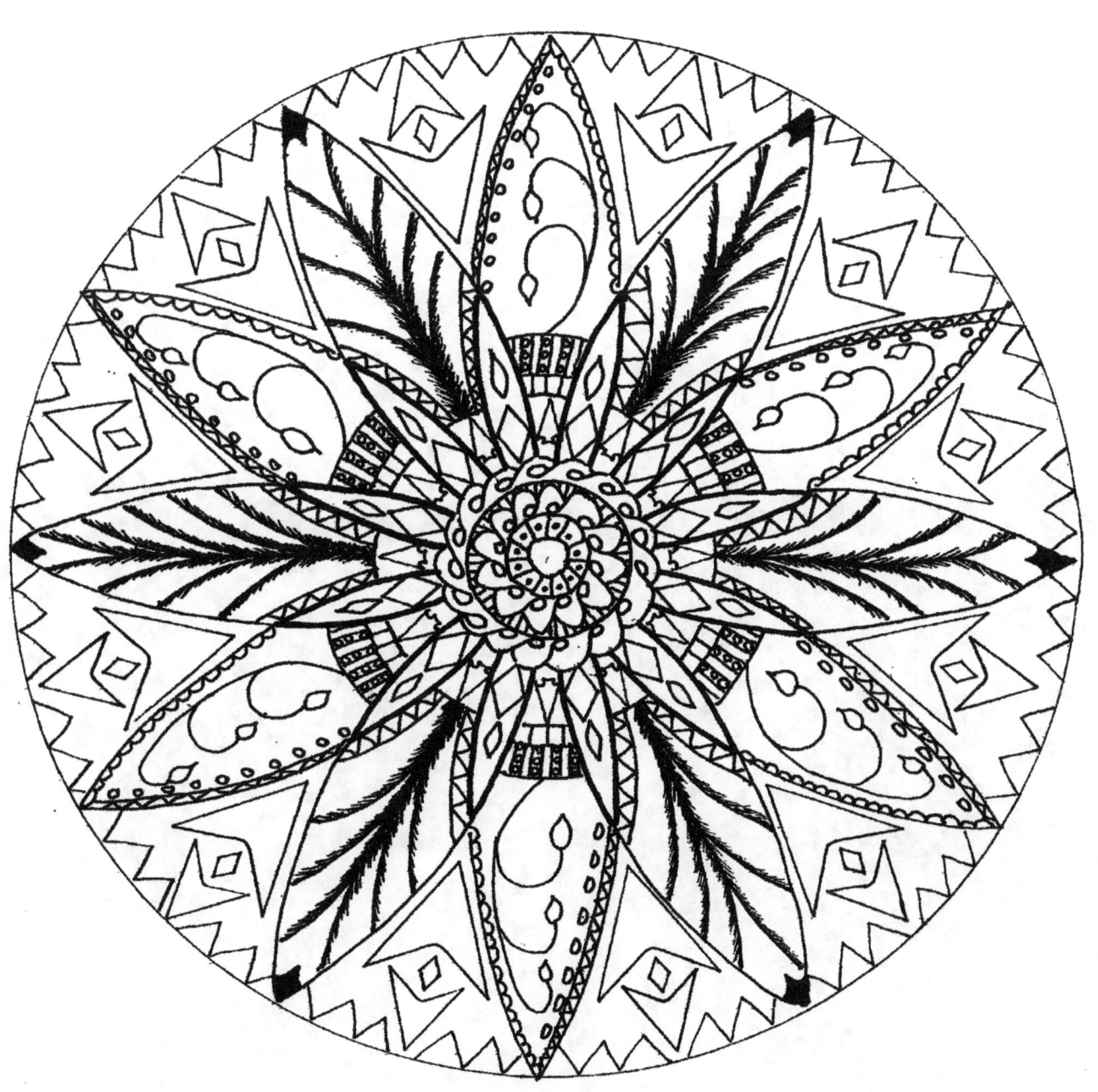

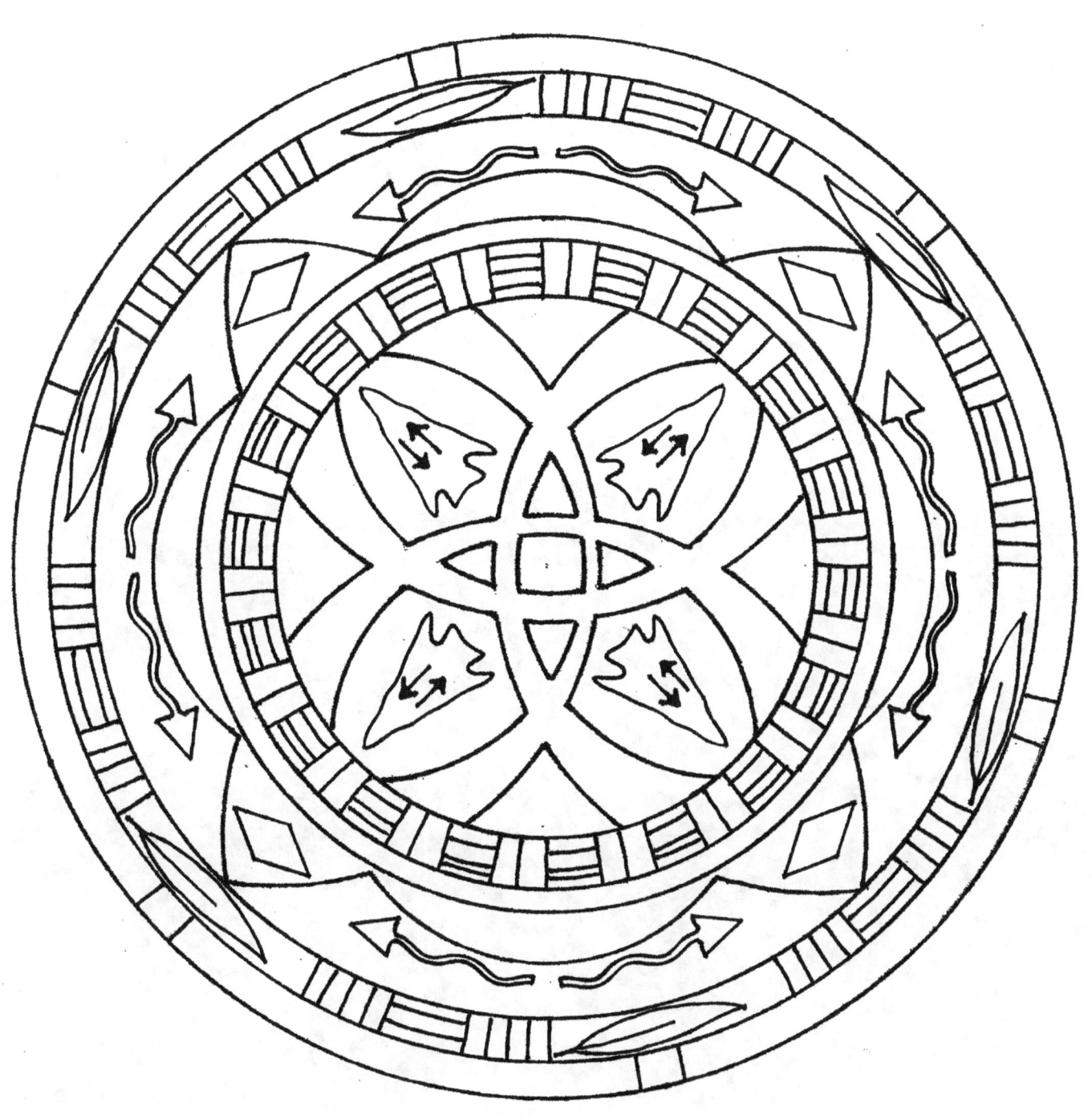

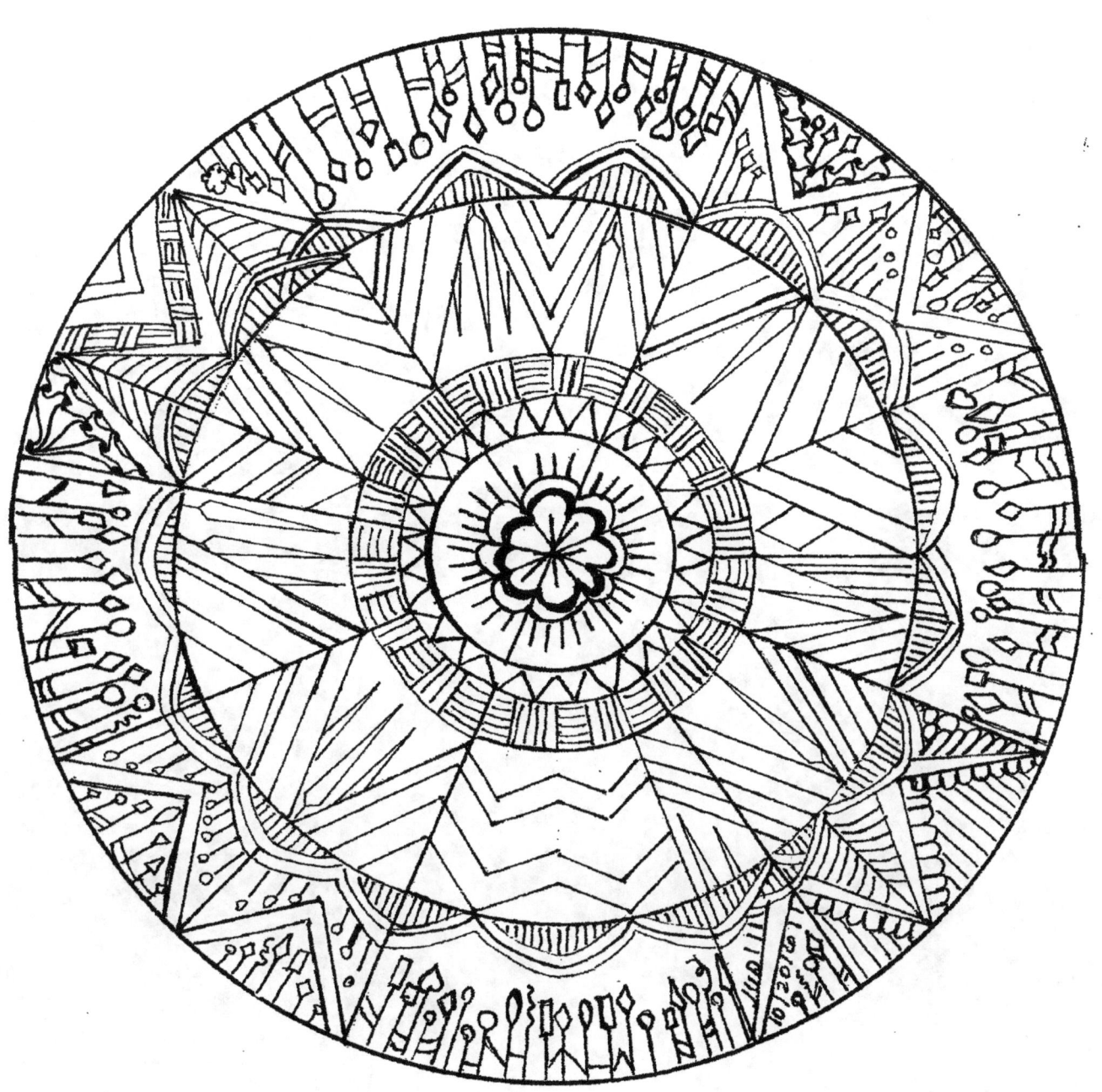

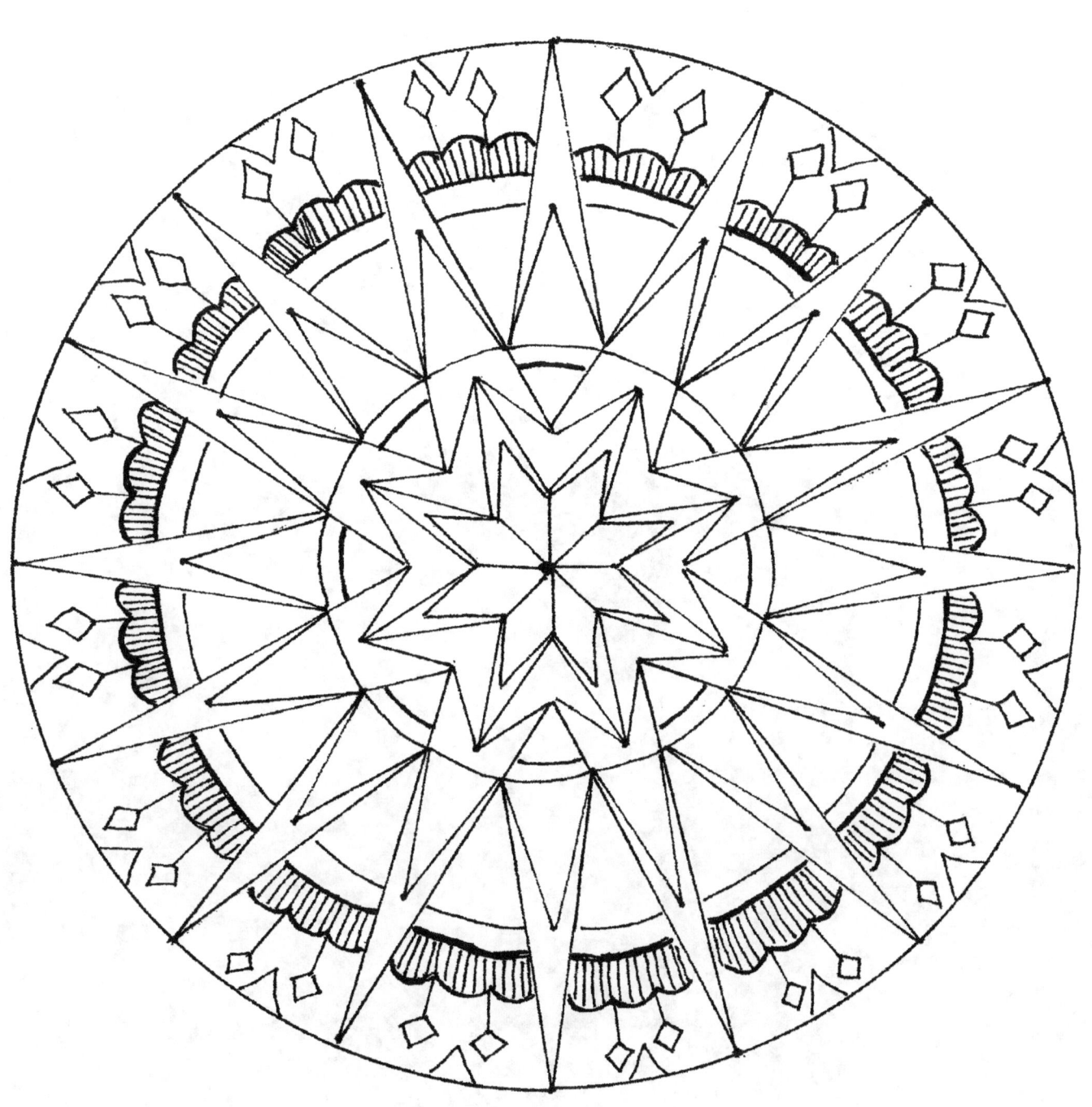

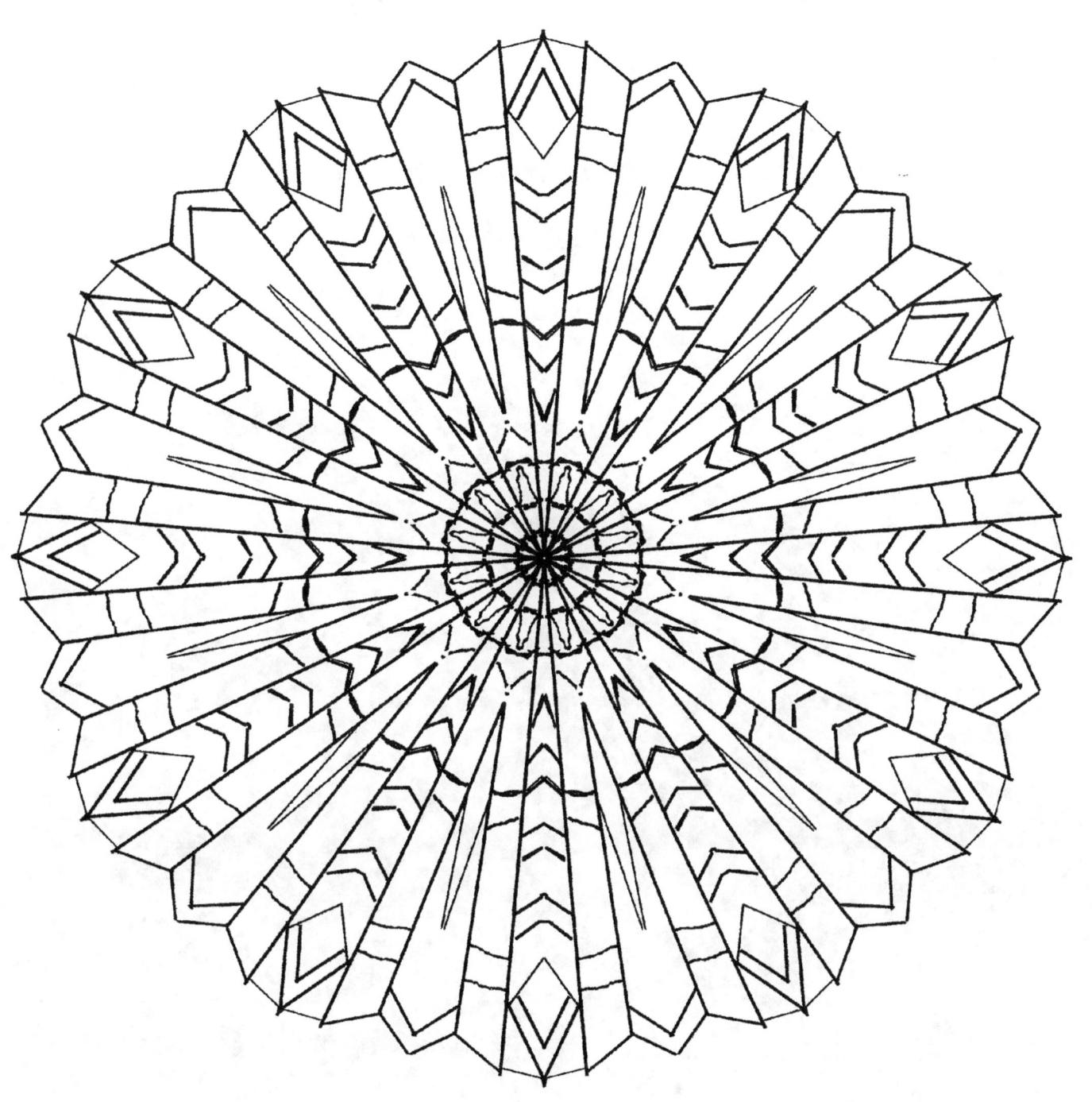

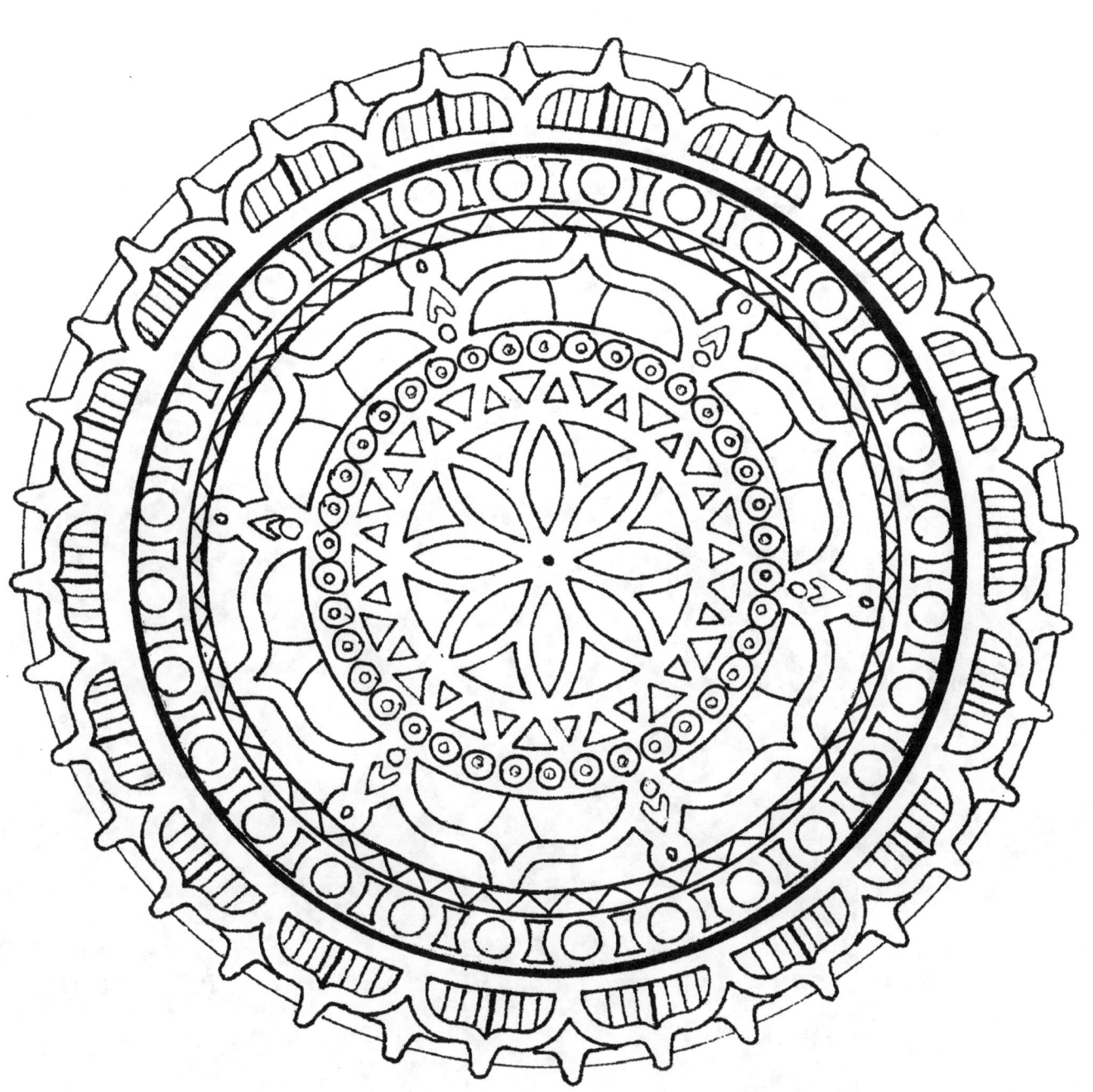

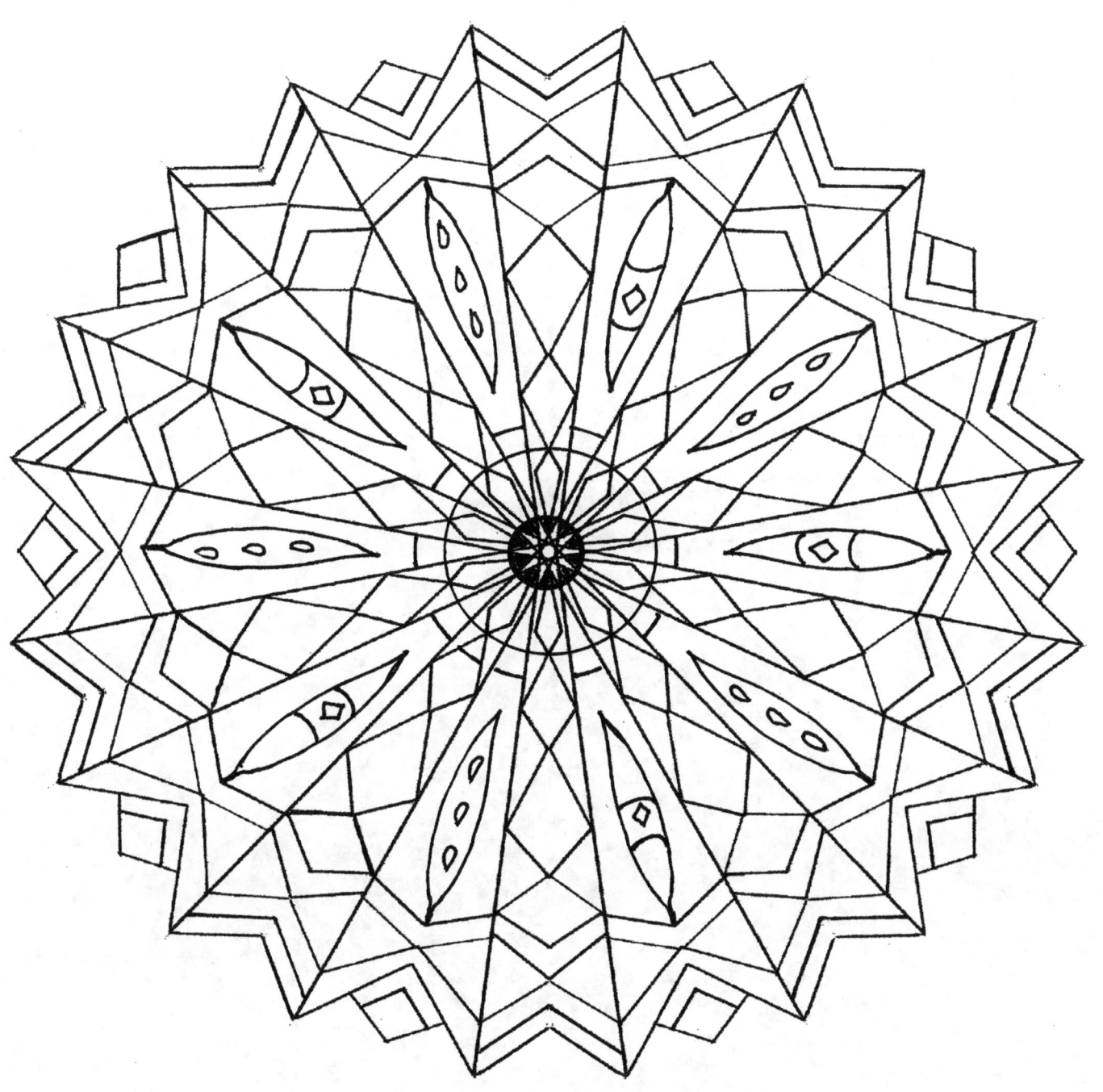

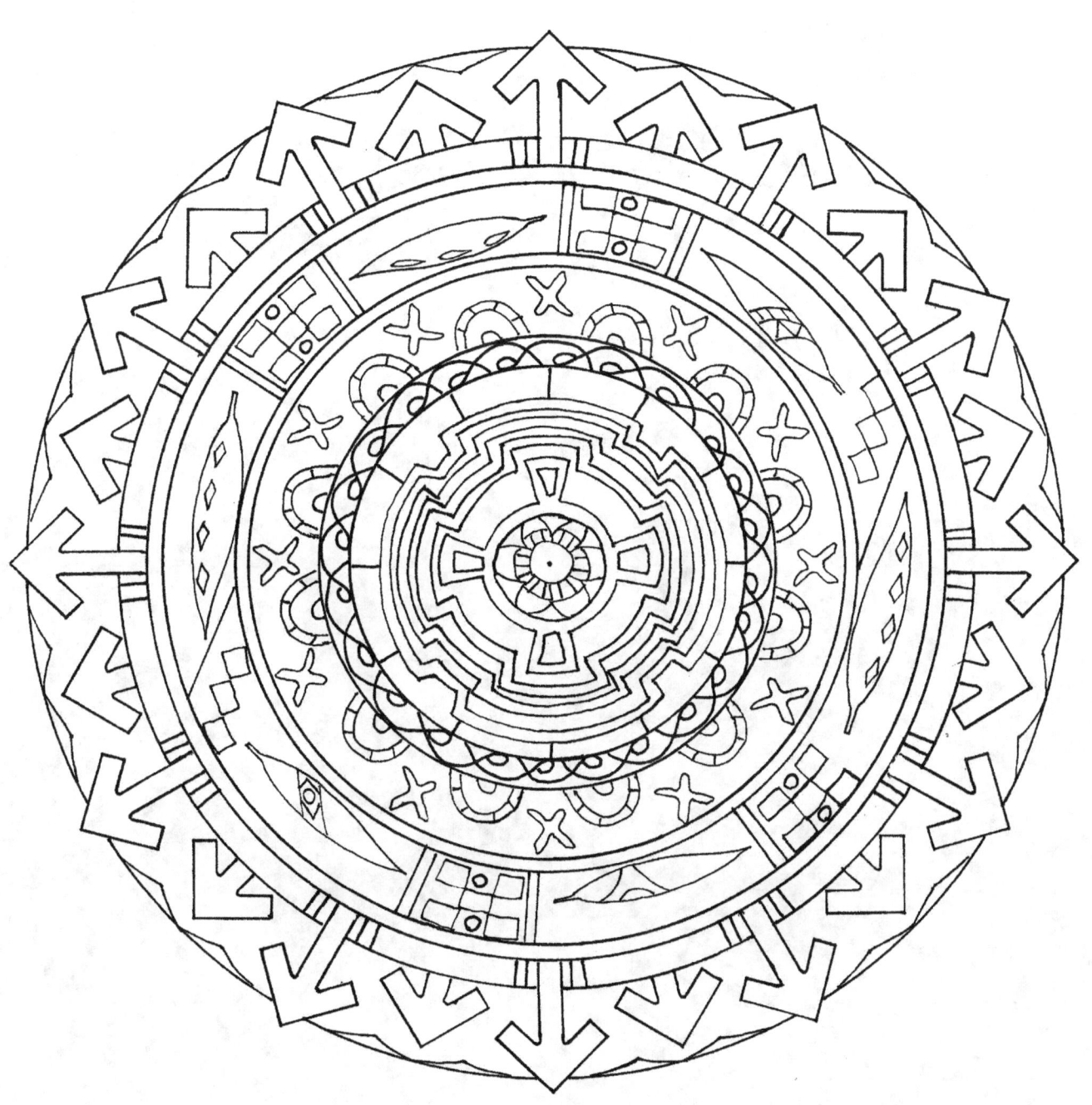

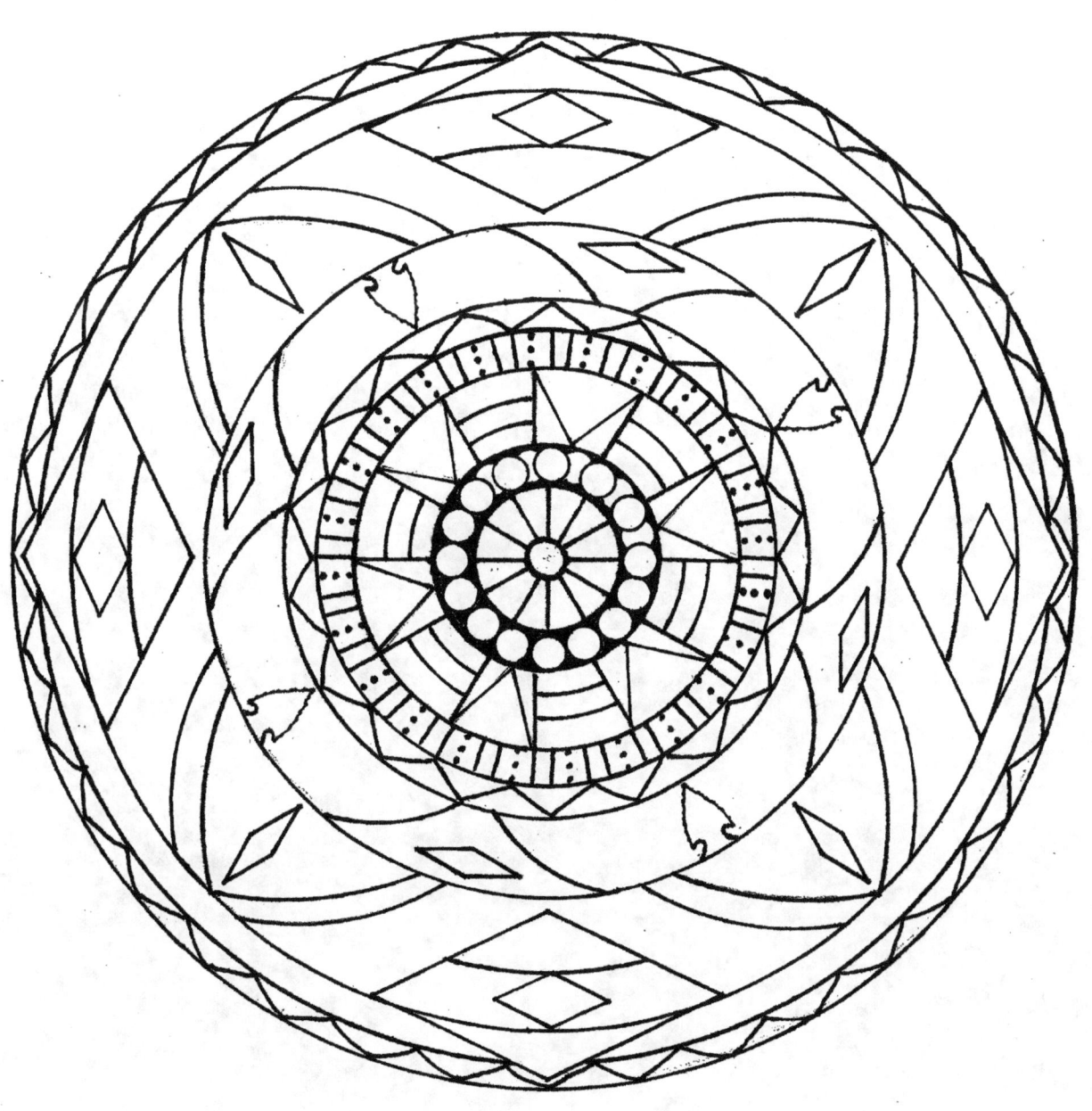

The following pages are simple mandala patterns or grids so that you may try your hand at designing your own mandalas.

Enjoy and have fun.

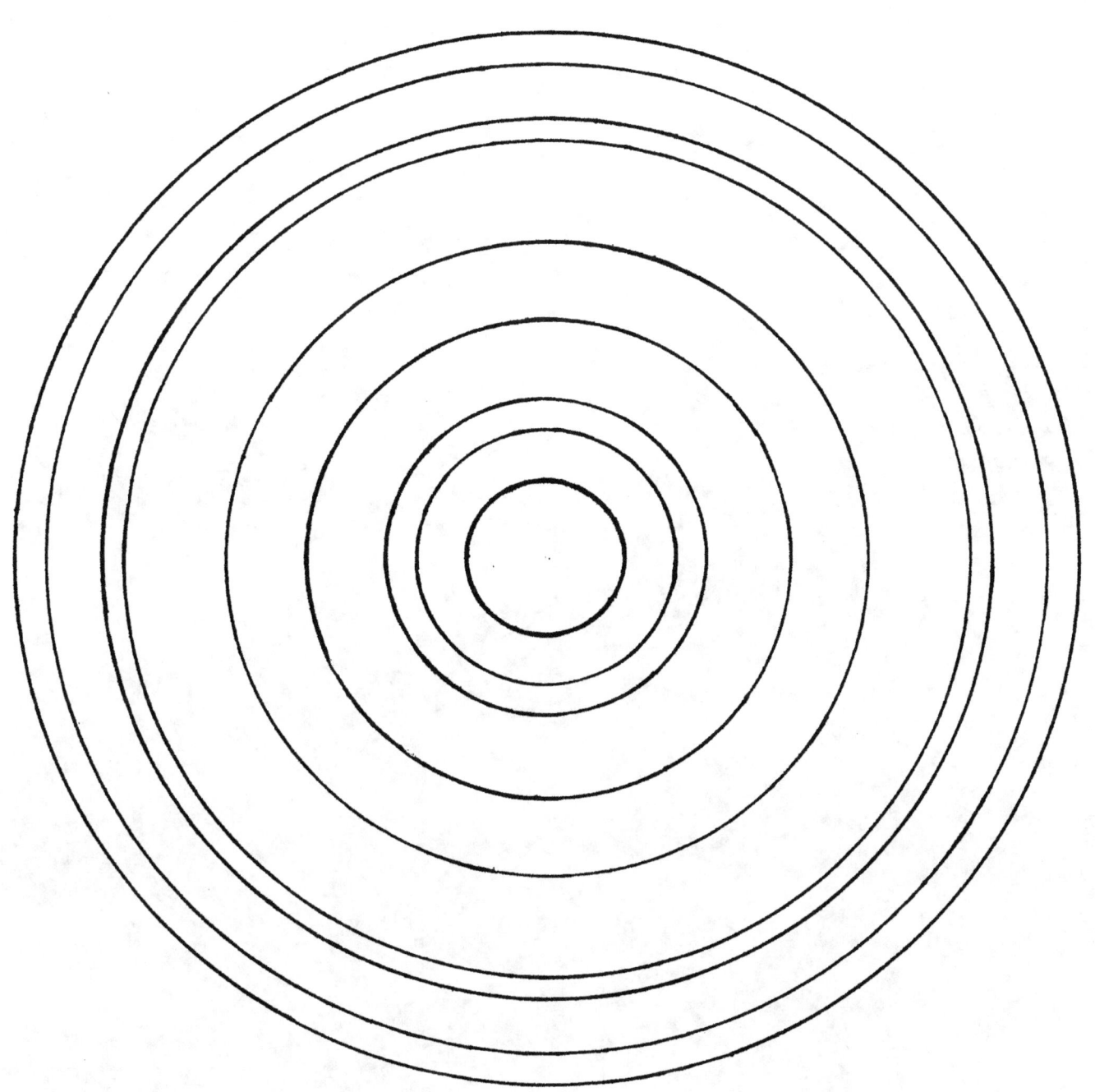

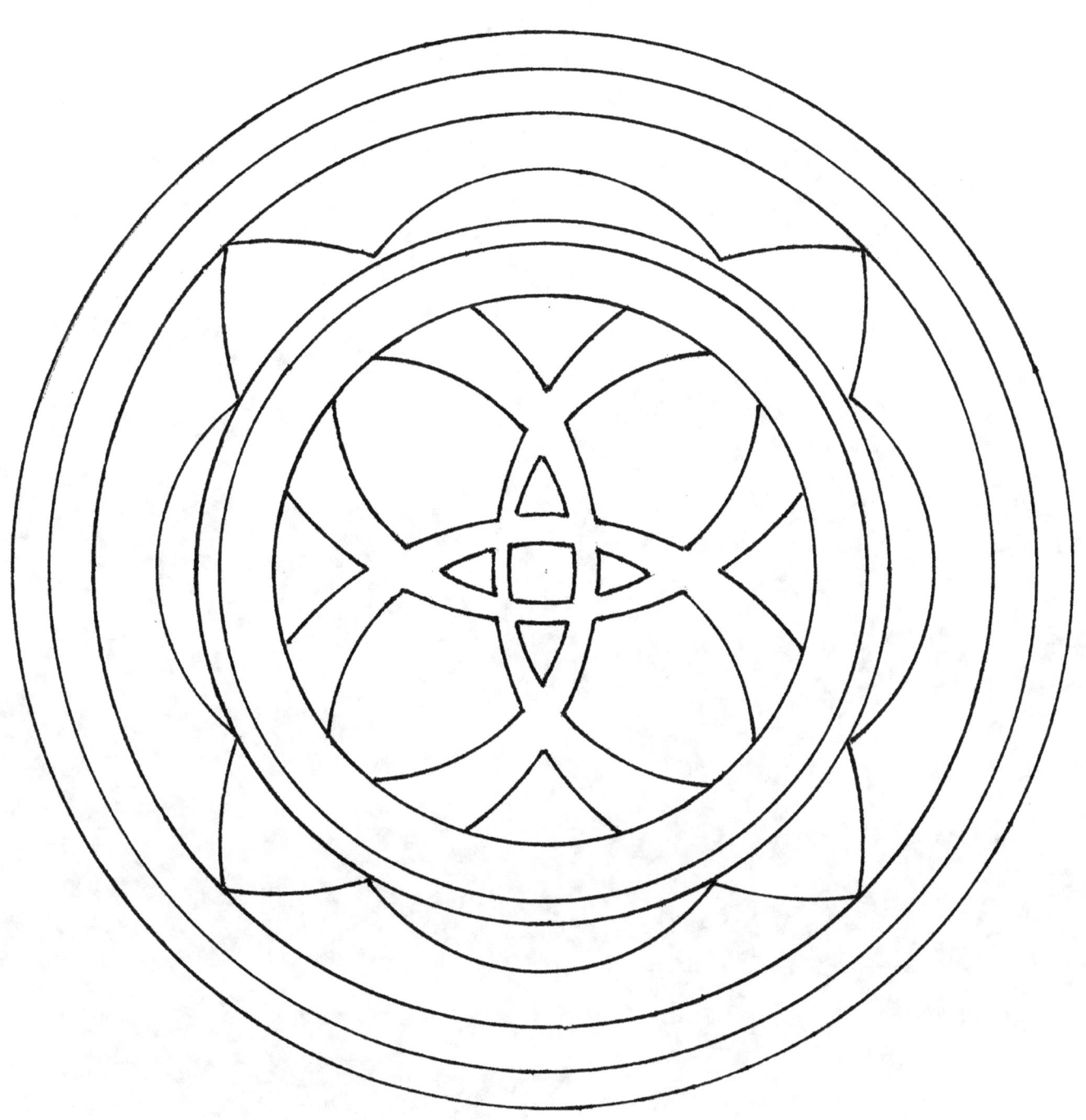

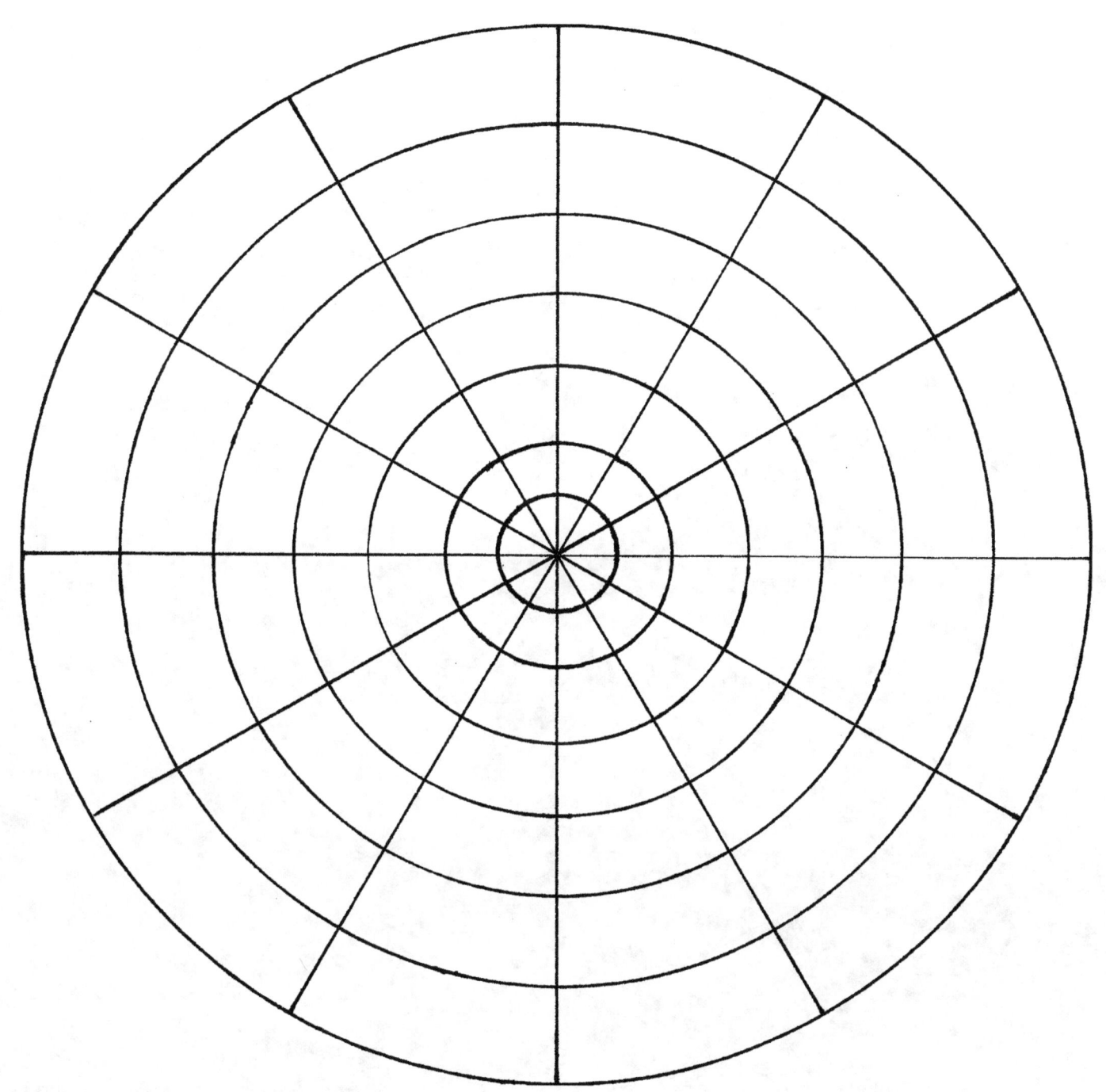

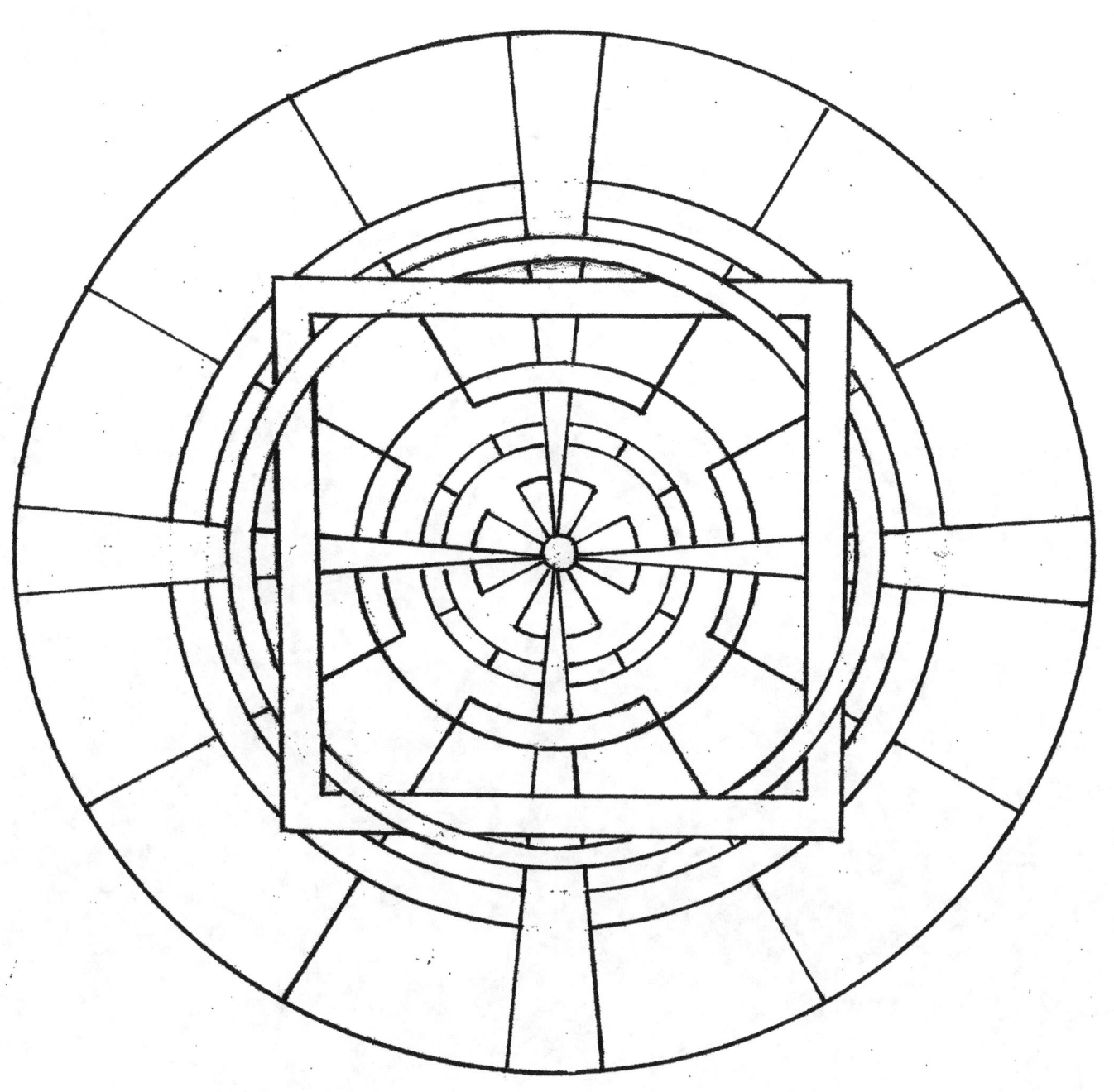

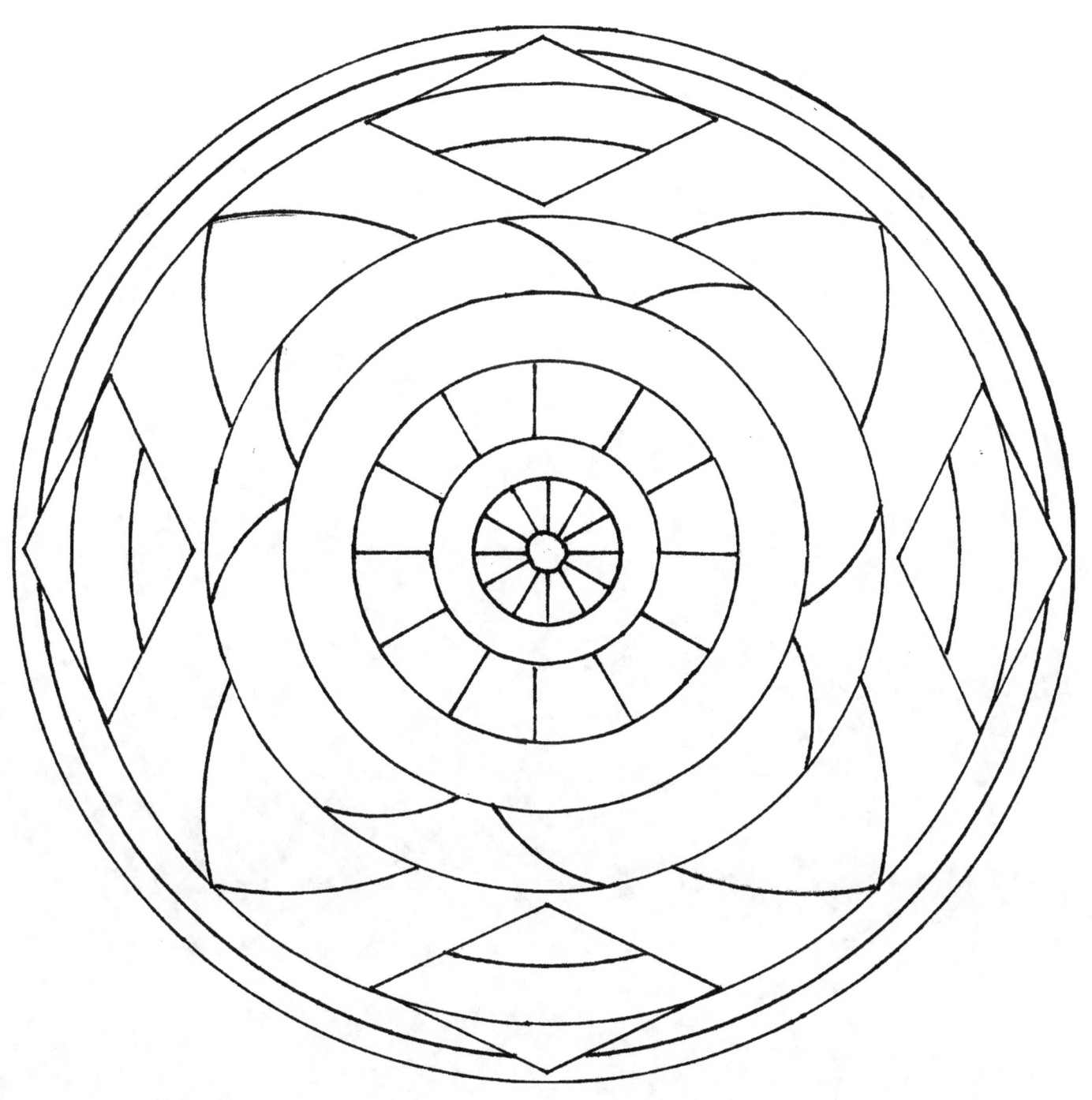

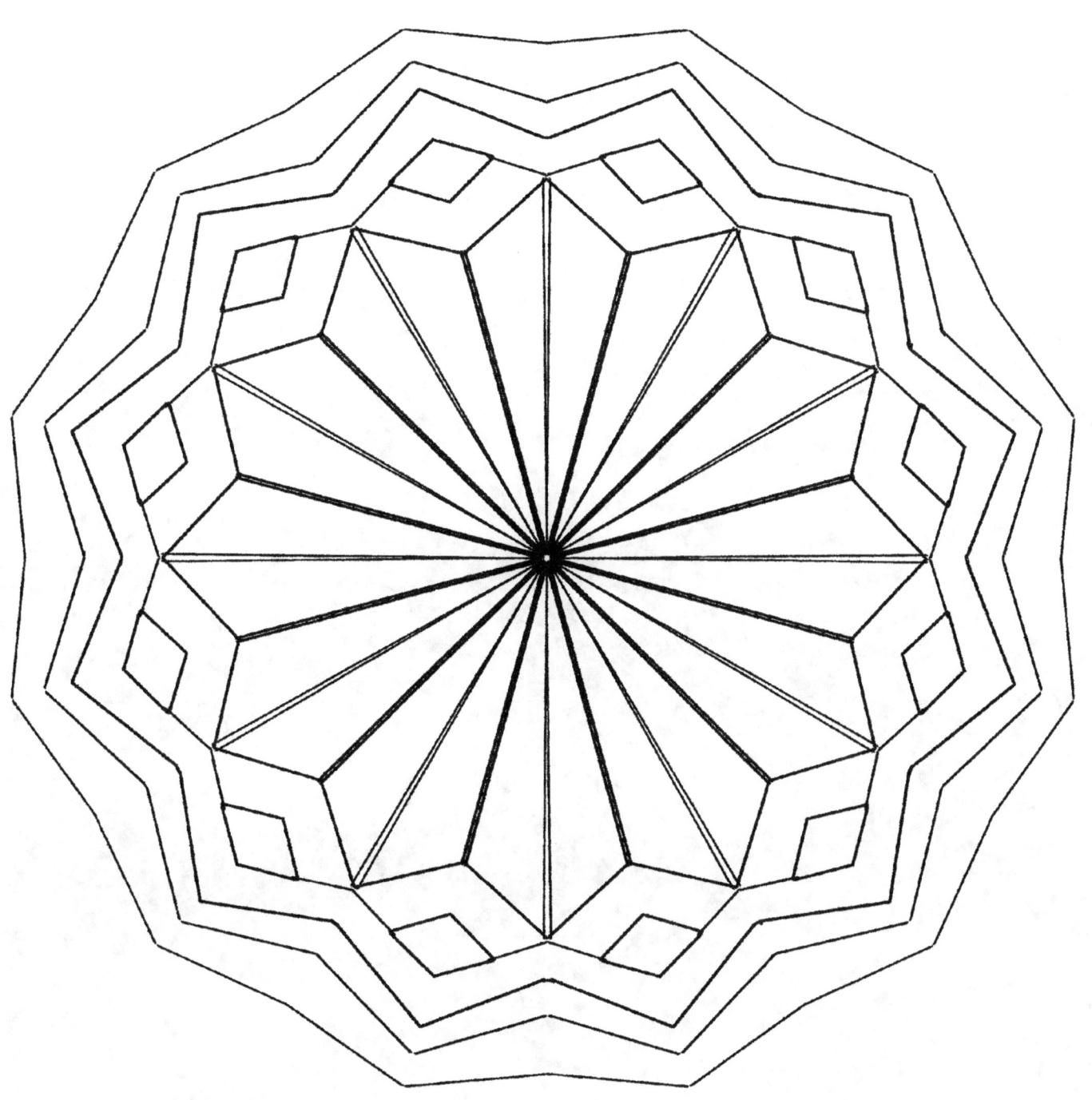

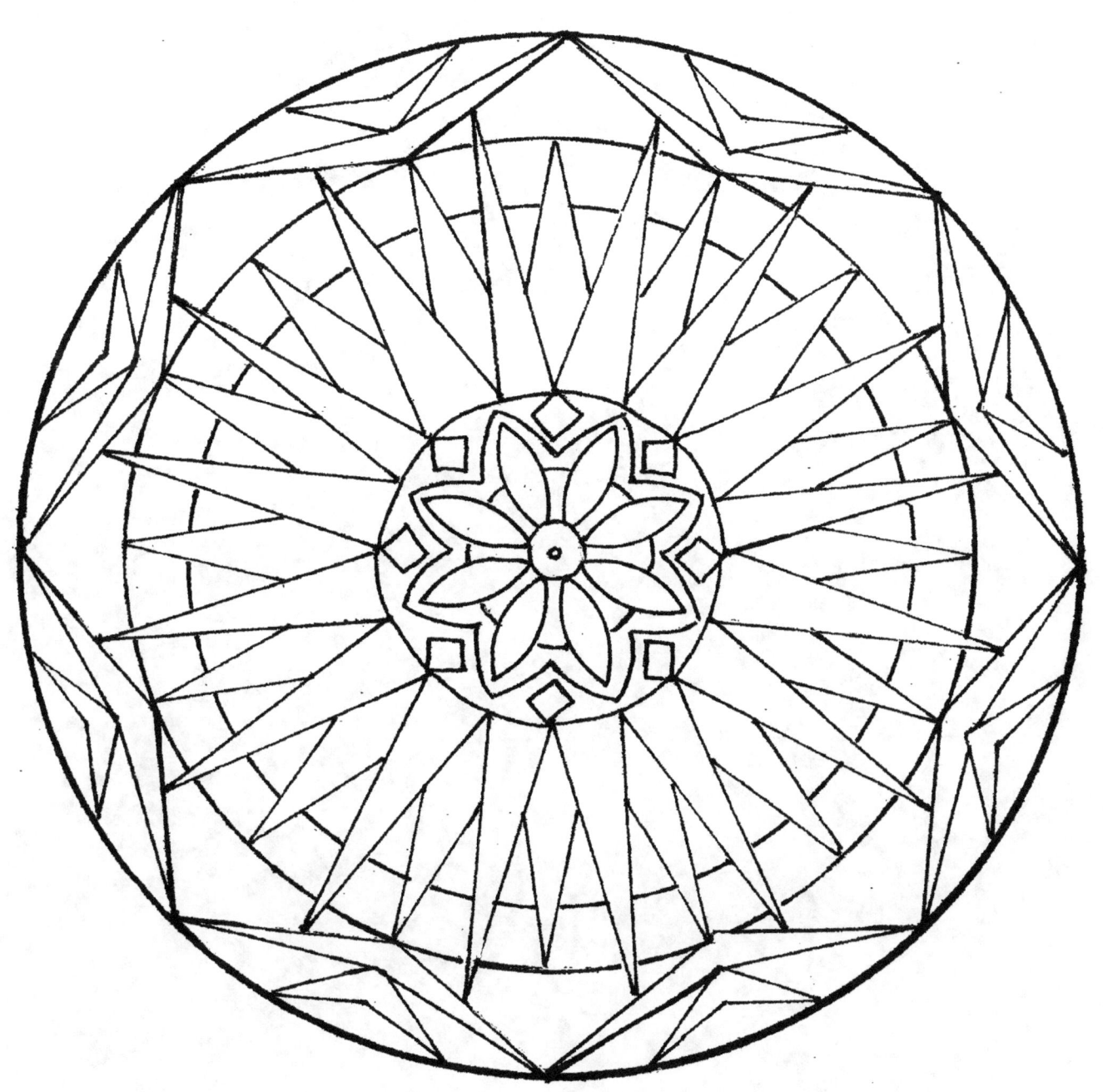

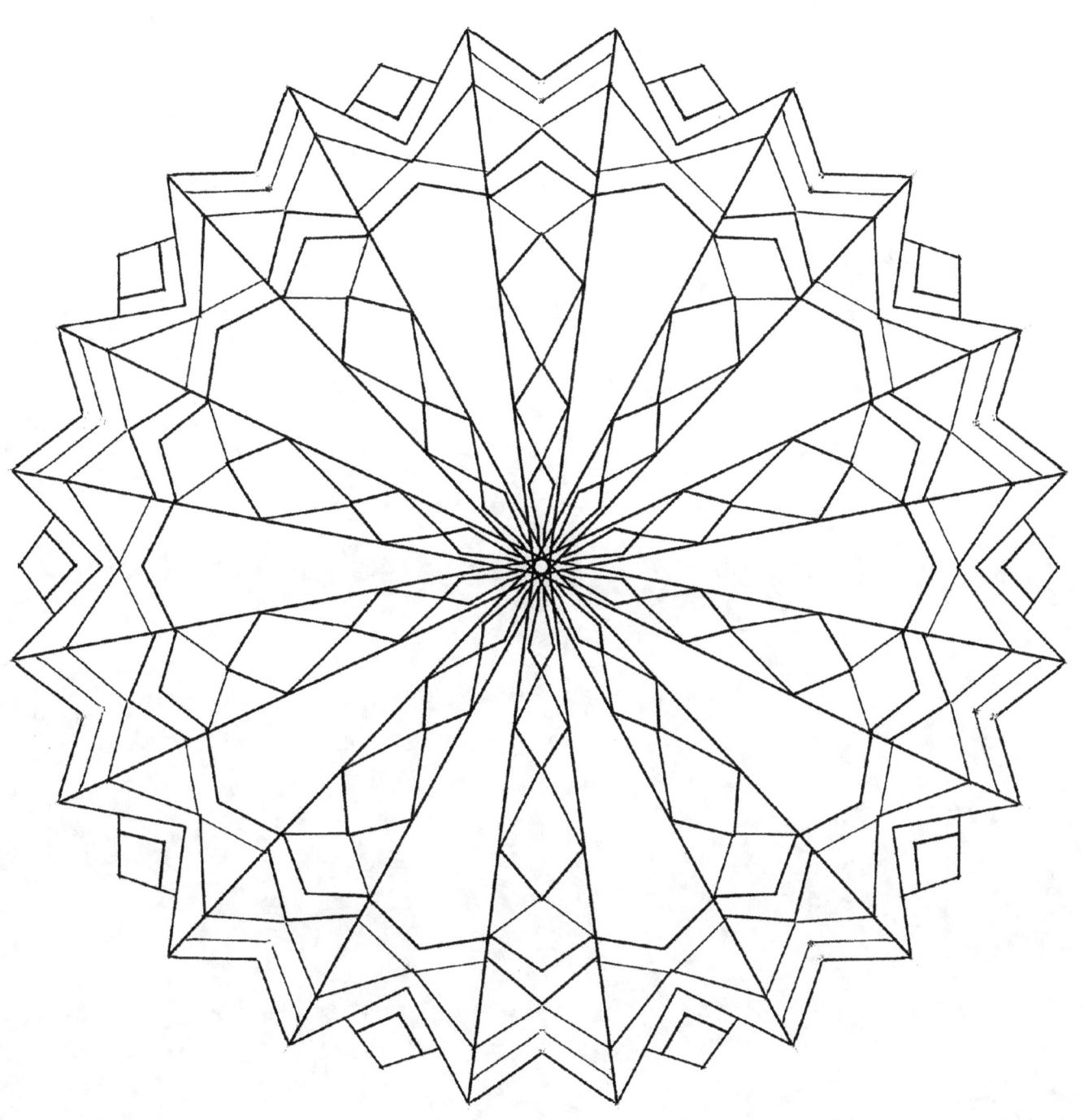